"Michael Tobin is one of Britain's most s[...] business leaders. His new book *Forget Stra[...] vations, tips and ideas for leaders in th[...] opening – when Tobin turns up for an a[...] wearing a tee shirt and ripped jeans, only to discover it is a black-tie dinner – to swimming with sharks, a KGB-type interrogation or hiking an Icelandic glacier, *Forget Strategy* is about thinking differently. Even if you disagree with some of what Tobin has to say, the stories will stick in the mind. An inspirational must-read for anyone who wants to think through problems and find inventive solutions."

Gavin Esler, BBC Presenter

"Michael Tobin avoids the traps of many management books and flies in the face of conventional wisdom. Focussing on EQ, his leadership approach delivers outstanding business performance and is equally relevant to an entrepreneur, someone taking their first steps into employment or a seasoned manager."

James Bennet, MBE, Director, Ernst & Young LLP

"This is a concise and effective manual for personal and commercial success, penned by a friend who has 'been there and done it' privately and publically. One of his mantras, '*Fear of failure closes you up. Feeling you have the power to change, to do something, is powerful. Don't worry about mistakes*' has driven his amazing business success and his remarkable and generous private life where he has helped so many, less fortunate than him. Read, learn the lessons, and execute them."

Alastair Stewart, OBE

"Mike is a great person, an inspiration to so many and has created success for himself and his companies through hard work, dedication and being brave enough to make tough decisions when they're needed which is vital as a leader. Despite his rise to the top, he has remained humble throughout and stuck to his core values, which is so important. A book worth reading if success and how to face up to challenges is what you're after."

Alec Stewart, OBE, Director of Cricket, Surrey CCC

"There is one thing of which I am certain. *'Doing good is good for business'* and that just shines through in everything that Tobin does. He has one of the biggest hearts I know in business and that translates into customer and staff loyalty. It can also alter perceptions from hard-nosed analysts like me. I learnt a lot from this book. Not just about Tobin but it also made me rethink my own personal approach to business. I suspect it will for you too."

Richard Holway MBE, Chairman, TechMarketView LLP

"It's amazing how Michael Tobin takes us through his own experiences to enlighten true fundamentals of leadership. It's a must-have book for any CEO."

Miquel Lladó, Professor of General Management, IESE Business School

"*Forget Strategy. Get Results.* differs from the 'traditional' management books I have read in the past. Tobin is direct and the 'F' themes are a useful guiding principle through the book. Certainly some of the practices are really valid and you'll likely find yourself relating to some based on your own experiences, either as a leader or a follower."

Carlos P. Hornstein, Head of US Executive Education, IESE Business School

"Pacey, direct, challenging and very well written."

Professor Susan Blackmore, Psychologist, freelance writer, lecturer and broadcaster

FORGET STRATEGY.
GET RESULTS.

RADICAL MANAGEMENT ATTITUDES THAT WILL DELIVER OUTSTANDING SUCCESS

MICHAEL TOBIN

WILEY

This edition first published 2014
© 2014 Michael Tobin

Registered office
John Wiley and Sons Ltd, The Atrium, Southern Gate, Chichester, West Sussex,
PO19 8SQ, United Kingdom

For details of our global editorial offices, for customer services and for
information about how to apply for permission to reuse the copyright material
in this book please see our website at www.wiley.com.

The right of the author to be identified as the author of this work has been
asserted in accordance with the Copyright, Designs and Patents Act 1988.

All rights reserved. No part of this publication may be reproduced, stored in
a retrieval system, or transmitted, in any form or by any means, electronic,
mechanical, photocopying, recording or otherwise, except as permitted by the UK
Copyright, Designs and Patents Act 1988, without the prior permission of the
publisher.

Wiley publishes in a variety of print and electronic formats and by print-on-
demand. Some material included with standard print versions of this book may
not be included in e-books or in print-on-demand. If this book refers to media
such as a CD or DVD that is not included in the version you purchased, you may
download this material at http://booksupport.wiley.com. For more information
about Wiley products, visit www.wiley.com.

Designations used by companies to distinguish their products are often claimed
as trademarks. All brand names and product names used in this book and on
its cover are trade names, service marks, trademark or registered trademarks of
their respective owners. The publisher and the book are not associated with any
product or vendor mentioned in this book. None of the companies referenced
within the book have endorsed the book.

Limit of Liability/Disclaimer of Warranty: While the publisher and author have
used their best efforts in preparing this book, they make no representations or
warranties with the respect to the accuracy or completeness of the contents of this
book and specifically disclaim any implied warranties of merchantability or fitness
for a particular purpose. It is sold on the understanding that the publisher is not
engaged in rendering professional services and neither the publisher nor the
author shall be liable for damages arising herefrom. If professional advice or other
expert assistance is required, the services of a competent professional should be
sought.

A catalogue record for this book is available from the Library of Congress

A catalogue record for this book is available from the British Library.

ISBN 978-1-118-80878-8 (paperback)   ISBN 978-1-118-80883-2 (hardback)
ISBN 978-1-118-80881-8 (ebk)   ISBN 978-1-118-80880-1 (ebk)

Cover design: Salad Creative Ltd
Set in 12/18pt MinionPro-Regular by Toppan Best-set Premedia Ltd, Hong Kong
Printed in Great Britain by TJ International Ltd, Padstow, Cornwall, UK

To my wife Shalina, whose "leap of faith" has given me
happiness beyond measure

To Daniel

Best regards

Mike JR

Richmond

June 16.

CONTENTS

INTRODUCTION

"This book is about experiences that have stuck with me and ideas that have influenced my life. What I have learned has enabled me to empower and inspire people around me – people far brighter than I will ever be – to perform fabulous things. I am riding the waves of change."

Often it takes someone else to point out that maybe you do things a little differently to other people. Because the way we behave in our life on a daily basis is – from our own point of view – simply the way we are.

A couple of years ago, I was trying to get back to London for an industry awards ceremony: I had been nominated as Personality of the Year, and the organizers were very keen for me to be there. I had taken a few days off to go skiing in Switzerland with my kids and was planning to fly back for the ceremony. As luck would have it, on the day itself, the weather was against me and all the flights were delayed or cancelled. I phoned in to say it didn't look like I was going to be able to make it after all. "Please make it," was the message back. "We really need you to be here."

There was a break in the weather, eventually, and well behind schedule a flight managed to get off the ground while the weather window was – precariously – open. I landed in London and, with minutes to spare, a cab whisked me over to the Grosvenor House Hotel just in the nick of time. As I walked into the ballroom, which was full to bursting with industry colleagues in immaculate tuxedos and evening wear, heads turned as they clocked my T-shirt and ripped jeans. "It's black tie," hissed someone helpfully. "I know, I know, I couldn't help it," I muttered as I sat down at the table.

The awards were announced and, gratifyingly, I had won the personality award I was up for. It was the main award of the night, and obviously explained why the organizers had been so insistent on my attendance. I made my way to the podium where the comedian Ed Byrne, who had been compering the event, made a suitably sardonic comment about my sartorial choice: "You could at least have made a f***ing effort." I joshed with him – "Hark who's talking!" – since he was looking pretty scruffy too. We all laughed and the evening moved on. But the impact of that lasted a long time. I was, from then on, remembered as the guy in the ripped jeans who had picked up the main gong. And people thought how daringly different I had been to go up and get the award like that. They didn't know it was entirely *faute de mieux*.

Although I had not planned to turn up to the event in ripped jeans, I had still been determined to be there no matter what, against all the odds – a commitment to honouring promises that has always been important to me – and then be prepared to take a certain amount flak and ridicule for standing out quite so obviously. It played in my favour, because that was what made me memorable.

These things stick. Ever since, I have been asked to talk about my approach to work, to business, to management, because other people perceive it as being somehow different, radical or creative.

For me it is just a natural way of operating. A management technique that has grown organically and imperceptibly out of the experiences of my life, and the way I view the world – a world that demands a new approach to business, where old-school, analogue management techniques are defunct. Where fast, flexible, fearless business thinking is the only way forward.

So when, following a merger between two companies who had been fierce competitors, I needed to diffuse the tensions between colleagues who had until recently been bitter rivals, I took them up to the Arctic Circle where they would have to huddle up together to keep each other's bodies warm to survive the night. When I wanted to encourage my team to break old patterns of thinking, I treated them to an unprotected swim with sharks to learn how to confront fear. To help key members of the company learn to field tough press enquiries I arranged for them to be "abducted" and "interrogated" on a trip to Tallinn.

Extreme? Maybe. Unusual? Definitely. Effective? Yes. Even if the way I run my business seems to others a little out of the ordinary, there is always a clear reason behind it, a result I have in mind, a purpose I am determined to aim for.

Although I was taught how to perform tricks by a member of the Magic Circle, there is no magic formula. No smoke and mirrors. No sleight of hand. My approach to business is grounded in real-life pain and toil, twinned with a little left-field imagination, plenty of business experience, and, I hope, a liberal dash of nous and gut feeling.

I always try to respect everyone, hurt no one and regret nothing. It is a kind of a mantra for me. The problem is that it is almost impossible to do all those things all the time. They end up conflicting with each other. But life for me is all about how we meander through those conflicts, making the tough decisions. Otherwise what's the point?

The strategies and attitudes in this book are, to me, instinctive, practical common sense driven by the realities of commercial life in the 21st century. They are applications of the core characteristics that underpin the philosophy I apply personally every day, and which I try to instil in the people who work with me. I want to encourage them to stand on "groundless ground;" to have the courage to believe in something when there are no logical grounds to assume they should. Our company operates in the ever-changing IT sector, and we are constantly having to predict, react and adapt to technological shifts that in turn impact directly on the way we will all live and work.

I am definitely not trying to set down in stone The Thoughts Of Chairman Michael (or of CEO Michael at least). The ideas in this book are meant to help you review and rethink the way you currently do your job or run your own business or team. They should provoke a questioning, querying, quizzical mindset. You may find it provocative. You may think it is outrageous in places. But, best of all, you don't even have to agree with me.

I didn't go to university. I don't have a brain the size of a planet, unlike many of the people I have the privilege to work alongside or do business with. But I do believe that by reflecting on your own experiences in the right way you can apply a new type of thinking to the way you operate in the future. And, because those experiences are personal to you, you will be better equipped with flexible optionality than you would be if you were to follow a set of hard and fast rules or theories.

That way you can take the decisions and the initiative in creating an experience, fostering an attitude, and developing a memory, a culture and a vision that directly inspire the business success of a company.

I have divided up the book into ten chapters, each centred on what I call an F Factor: from Freedom to Fortitude, Focus and Faith. Each starts with a story from my business life: a problem I had to deal with, the solution I devised and the positive outcome that followed. The F themes are the essential strands of my business DNA, and I hope you will come away with questions you can pose to yourself about your own approach, and which may prompt fresh ways of thinking.

One of my F Factors is Fun: however serious and pressurized your business, however difficult and unrelenting the economic climate or market conditions, always leave a sliver of space to have fun, as well as doing business in a way that makes you feel good. If we can all achieve that, I believe the world of industry and commerce will be a far better place.

1
FEAR

"I learnt early on in my life never to have regrets, to face the future whatever it was going to be, to make tough decisions by getting on and doing it."

The Problem: *The fear of fear itself*

It was the summer of 2006, the really hot one. As a major merger loomed between the company that I was running at the time – Redbus – and Telecity, one of our fiercest competitors, I knew that core members of my staff were getting increasingly nervous about who amongst them might be at risk of losing their jobs.

There was history between the two companies. Since the late 1990s they had been sworn enemies, battling to dominate the nascent market for data centre capacity. At times the fighting had been nothing less than cut-throat.

However, I had a vision that if Redbus and Telecity could only be brought together as one entity, the new company that emerged would be able to reshape the industry, by pulling in the same direction rather than expending energy locked in a bloody battle. Competition between companies is healthy, but it can also be exhausting.

After two years trying to engineer the merger, and three or four failed attempts, I was finally at the point where, barring last-minute or unseen problems, the merger was on the verge of happening.

But my team was understandably worried. Each member knew that in most mergers there are going to be two people for each job and, out of necessity, one of those people will have to be let go. It was a time of tough decisions and there was nervousness about who would get fired. It was exacerbated by the fact that those who lost their job would do so to someone from the rival company they had been up against, some of them for their entire career.

I could sense, practically smell, the fear in my key management team. It was distracting them from the functions they had to carry on doing in the meantime. I needed them to confront and overcome that fear.

The Solution: *Swimming with sharks*

I wanted to create an experience that would help the team convert their fearfulness into fear*less*ness, something that would instil fear in them but then show them that their fear was unfounded.

"We went off to swim with sharks. Face to face with an icon of danger. This would be confronting fear by being thrown in at the deep end."

We had, as we still do, a regular management meeting away from the office. On this occasion I booked us into a hotel in Edinburgh: we held a business meeting, talked about the future, and the merger. We also visited a local whisky museum and, one afternoon, I took them out towards the Forth Bridge, where the minibus turned into the Deep Sea World car park.

Everyone was relaxed, if somewhat puzzled. The first inkling they had of what I had in mind was when each of them was asked for their wetsuit sizes. I wasn't letting them in on anything. With the suits on, we all had breathing apparatus training. Already there was apprehension in the ranks. Some had never put a wetsuit on before, most had never used an aqualung. For a first-timer, the sensation of wearing the suit and the apparatus felt claustrophobic and very uncomfortable.

Once the training session was complete, I finally broke the news of what was ahead. "Listen up," I said, "you are all going to be swimming with sharks. Down on the seabed, inside a man-made aquarium, but with no cages, no Plexiglas protection. Upfront and personal." That was when the fear kicked in. It was palpable.

There were 13 of us on the outing. One of them had to be excused on medical grounds because he had a back problem. Fair enough. Four simply said they were too scared and were insistent they couldn't do it. I didn't try to railroad them, but left them to make up their own minds. While they thought about it, the others were being taken, two by two, into the water by the instructors. There was a five-minute swim down to the seabed, just long enough to get really frightened. Then you saw the sharks.

These were big beasts. Three-metre-long hammerheads and tiger sharks. When it was my turn the anticipation on the way down was definitely unpleasant but, once I was down there, I felt much better. It was extraordinary to be this close to the sharks. They swam right up to me, out of curiosity, but – well-fed by their handlers in advance – they were not looking for a little lunch. "Just don't put your hands out to touch them," we had been advised. I hoped everyone would remember that because there was no insurance and I didn't want to lose anyone from the management team before I absolutely had to (and the danger was real – some years later there was an incident at the same centre when a staff diver was bitten by an angel shark).

As the groups of two went down, those left waiting their turn had an exquisitely painful time. They could watch each pair swimming down, then see them coming back out of the water – some absolutely buzzing with the wow factor, others just glad to be out of there, though still exhilarated. In the end everyone swam, bar one.

The Outcome: *Emerging from the challenge*

Once the shark dive was finished, we all went out to dinner. I asked everyone what they had felt when they realized what was in store. One guy said he had been excited, that it was something he had always wanted to do. Most of the others said they had felt a huge panic. Everyone admitted to having been terrified – regardless of the fact that the instructors diving with them had assured them it would be fine. Nothing the shark specialists said had alleviated a primeval fear.

And what about when they were on the seabed? That was still terrifying, they said, but nowhere near as terrifying as the anticipation and apprehension. As the seconds and then minutes ticked by and the sharks were only staring, not attacking, they had realized that what the instructors said was true. They started adjusting their expectations.

"And what did you feel when you came out?" I asked. "It was a life-changing experience." "I was overcome. I dealt with something that I didn't even know was an issue."

The shark swimming experience became embedded as part of company folklore. At my wedding in 2012, more than five years later, I had four best men, three of whom were part of the team who had been on that swim. And all of them mentioned it in their speeches.

That experience taught the whole team that it is easier to confront the reality than to dwell in apprehension.

The merger took place, and it was successful: the two main European rivals became the clear market leader, and subsequently had the critical mass to transform the data centre industry completely. Telecity turnover grew by over 350% in the following seven years.

My decision to go swimming with sharks was not macho posturing on my part, or just an excuse for a gimmicky awayday. Strangely, whenever I talk about the swim, people simply don't believe we did it. But it's true. I've got the photos to prove it. I talk about the sequence of dealing with initial, massive fear, moving to a phase of fear blended with excitement, and the life-changing exhilaration that follows. And, by reaching that final stage of exhilaration, you know that you can handle all the fear that went before. And they still insist, "No, you didn't do that . . ."

I didn't do this because I thought it would be a good story to tell. It had a genuine purpose, which led to a real impact on the people who took part, and was in turn an element of the ethos in the new company.

* *

If, by the way, you are not familiar with the data centre industry, here is a succinct explanation. A recent *New Statesman* focus on the industry put it this way: "A data centre is a building (or self-contained unit within a building) used to house computing equipment such as servers along with associated components such as telecommunications, network and storage systems." Data centres handle vast quantities of digital data (and data has been described by McKinsey's Dennis Layton as "the iron ore for a new industrial revolution"), and play a vital part in the way our digital world operates, like a brain at the very centre of the global digital network.

No fear?

There was a best-selling business book in the 1980s, written by the American businessman Harvey Mackay, called *Swim With The Sharks Without Being Eaten Alive: Outsell, Outmanage, Outmotivate and Outnegotiate Your Competition*. It was published in the era of Gordon Gekko, dog eat dog (or in Gekko-speak, "If you want a friend, get a dog"), ruthless, money-driven competitiveness. My swimming with sharks message is not about becoming a shark. Those days are over. It is about dealing with fear.

I believe that it is vital to learn how to remove the fear factor from business. That doesn't mean denying that fear exists. I still experience many fears. But to progress, grow and build, you have to channel fear, and make that change from fearful to fearless. Let's explore what that means in a business environment.

Address fear by accepting it as inevitable

Accept uncertainty as a fact of business life. If you are going to deliver more in business, you are going to have to head outside your comfort zone. Good business, successful business, demands the ability to encounter and confront tough business issues and decisions.

Hunkering down inside that comfort zone used to be the safe option – in the current climate, staying put and keeping your head down is no longer a guarantee of a natty gold watch on your retirement day. Nothing is guaranteed. Job security is an archaic concept. Progress involves poking your head above the parapet, taking a risk.

This is ever more important. We are living, working, succeeding or failing in a new environment, in which technology is changing at the fastest rate in history. We are living in an exponential world. There is no time for techno-fear: Carly Fiorina, the former CEO of Hewlett-Packard, has said, "The past 25 years have been the warm-up act. We are now entering the era in which technology will truly transform every aspect of business, government, education and society of life." From the point of view of the IT sector, this is not only true but it will remain true for the foreseeable future.

The funny thing is, whoever is reading this book will have had x number of years' experience behind them, where they worried and pondered many times about many things. Funnily enough they are still sitting here reading this book. So they have got through all of those things. It is almost like inviting someone to go back in their mind and think about when they were really worried about something, desperately worried, and yet here they are. The sun keeps on coming up and you somehow get through it. And that goes back to the sharks.

Maybe that was a particularly extreme excitement, but often in daily life it doesn't have to be that extreme. You are enjoying yourself; take the time to appreciate that you are enjoying yourself.

Be prepared to make bold career moves

There has been a fear factor in every job I have taken on, every career decision I have made. I have always gone in way beyond my own comfort zone.

At each stage, other people have confidently told me I had no chance of getting the job I was going for, or achieving the targets I set for myself and others. Impossible? No way. I constantly took on what looked like ridiculous challenges: moving across to run business in countries that were new to me and where I didn't even know the language. At the age of 21 I was appointed MD of a French tech company. I didn't speak French. But I knew I could learn it there. I arrived in Paris the weekend before starting the job, without an apartment. The prospect was daunting. The potential for being frozen with fear was high. I didn't know any better so I got on with it. Maybe I'm just bolshy by nature. But I prefer to think of it as being fearless.

Convert fear into a positive excitement about future possibilities

How can you pass on that sense of not being afraid of fear to colleagues? One of the most common examples I come across is with those who have specific targets to achieve. Let's say they need to achieve £1 million in sales and, at the moment, with the year end approaching all too fast, it looks like they will fall short by a quarter of a million. In most companies they will be feeling afraid, fearful of what that "failure" to achieve an agreed target might mean in terms of their career, job security, peer pressure.

I try to encourage them to step outside the fear, by telling them, "You are already a success for achieving 75%+ of your target. Now set yourself a higher target – get rid of your fear of not making that 100% because you don't need to be afraid. Go out there, and get me 105% – and by taking that ridiculously challenging opportunity and making it successful, when no one else could think you would do it, you will be a hero. Choose that outcome and then go back and find the building blocks you need to make it."

Appreciate the excitement of doing something that scares you

Rather than worrying about the prospect of leaving your comfort zone, remember the buzz that everyone on my team felt after swimming with the sharks. Embrace the fear and enjoy the feeling of conquering it. This is the art of converting distress into de-stress.

Many companies have experienced what has been called a "crucible moment," a tough, scary phase when everything could have gone disastrously wrong, but which the team survived and from which they emerged stronger, tempered like steel. They have taken tangible lessons away from nerve-wracking experiences and turned them into working practices and protocols.

Always take the lesson from every situation

The follow-on from that attitude is calmly analyzing every business situation you find yourself in – the good, the bad and the downright ugly – and drawing a lesson that you can apply in the future even if the situation is, on the surface, completely different.

I take a healthily sceptical view of the statistics and percentages that research projects throw up – I read a report recently that suggested more people feared public speaking than death, which may or not be true: it depended how the question was framed. But in the research into fear, there is one figure that makes sense to me: 40% of us fear the future. In other words, we fear what has not happened, and may very well never happen; we fear what does not exist. Another 40% of us worry about things that have happened, our fear is rooted in the past, which has gone and which we cannot now affect. So 80%, probably more, of fear and worry is wasting effort, emotion and energy on what we cannot affect. It is far better to concentrate on those aspects of business and home life that we can alter.

A pattern emerges: by driving through the element of fear, by being prepared to go way beyond your comfort zone, by looking at things that most people would see as a risk as an opportunity, you can create the kind of luck that drives opportunity. Convert fear into a positive excitement about future possibilities.

In essence, do not fear what you do not know. Expect the uncertain to be full of fear but it is likely to be less than you expect. Enjoy it because it will be a learning experience.

"Nothing in life is to be feared, just understood."

Marie Curie

Taking it back to basics

There was a point in my career where I was based in Denmark as part of ICL. I had been sent there to turn around ICL's main-frame service and repair company into an outsourcing managed services division. It was going well and, as a result, I was picked out to become part of what ICL called the Millennium Pro-gramme: this was in the late 1990s.

ICL had about 60,000 employees worldwide and they had chosen a group of 25 from their companies across the globe to be prepared and cultivated as potential Corporate Board members of the future. They had scoured the workforce, sourced us from different countries and different functions, and brought us all together.

The programme involved us spending a week or more every month on the programme for a whole year. It was a stunning idea: all these people with significant P&L and other responsibilities being taken out for a week every month of their very difficult challenges and put together in the group. Of course we all thought we were the golden boys and girls.

Then, what did they do? First, we were broken up into five teams of five. We had already completed a set of psychometric tests and multiple Q&As so they had already built a profile of us with a raft of characterizations. A psychologist joined each group. In my particular group, she proceeded to rip the heart out of everybody.

When it came to me she said, "So when you were about seven years old I suppose your mum and dad broke up, did they?" "Yes, but how did you know that?" "Well, you demonstrate clear traits of x, y, z. Not only that but I would imagine this was also part of your past."

She was telling me more about myself than I could have even written down for them, by drawing my profile out of the analysis of my character.

She ruined me in front of the other four in my group, and then did the same to everyone else. And when everyone was in tears, she said, "OK, guys, for each of you, the other four are going to tell you how you can improve yourself." And we went round the table in turn.

One of the others was a sales director in a particular territory. All he wanted to do was run the local subsidiary, but his boss had been in place for time immemorial and showed no signs of moving. The advice we gave him, having heard his story, was "Leave, go and get a job with another company." Within the context of the Millennium Programme, which was meant to find future leaders for ICL, this was very dangerous advice; but they were prepared to encourage it and, two months later, that colleague was gone. He got in touch and said, "Thanks guys. I took your advice, and I am now so happy."

This was the point: the process broke us all down to a base level where everyone was nothing, and we could see that we had all experienced the same major issues and challenges, from child-hood onwards. We had nothing to prove any more, we had gone beyond the fear of being broken down in front of our colleagues and, consequently, we became open to absorbing new ideas and fresh learning.

We were completely open to all inputs. From that point they started to build us up again.

There is a time to let go

In 2012, I was on honeymoon in South Africa. I took my wife, Shalina, up Table Mountain. What I had not told her was that, as an extra element, I had secretly arranged for a team of paragliders to meet us at the summit. She gamely agreed to paraglide with an instructor off the mountain.

As we prepared, Shalina was strapped into a harness; the instructor behind her was also strapped into a harness with the large paraglide. In front of her another member of the paraglide team was just down the incredibly steep slope.

I looked round to see Shalina holding on for dear life to the guy in front of her. At that point, the fear of jumping off Table Mountain had kicked in. She would not let go of the paraglide team member in front of her, absolutely would not let go, because she thought that he represented her security.

In reality, he was less secure than she was. She was higher up the slope, strapped to an instructor and supported by the giant wing. If a gust of wind had caught her, they would all be going down the mountain, only he would not have a sail. He was asking Shalina to let him go, because it was extremely dangerous. She was telling him she needed to hang on to something. Her mind, every instinct in her body, was not allowing her to think that holding onto him was even more dangerous for everyone concerned than just letting go. When she did steel herself to release her grip, she and her instructor soared high, spiraling out on an exhilarating ride.

Fear often creates hesitancy: most accidents on roundabouts are caused not by cars crashing into the side of each other but by people starting to pull out and then suddenly hesitating, so that the car behind shunts into the back of them. It is better to get onto the roundabout and, even if you are not sure which exit you need to take, going round a couple of times – being active, creating positive movement.

Either you do something about this issue that is causing you fear, even that smallest step, that first step of dealing with it; or, if there is nothing to do, then there's nothing to do, so why worry about it? It is going to happen. Normally you are afraid of things, of something specific, whereas worrying is almost like not knowing what you are afraid of, because it is a fear of what could happen but does not have to.

The song says "*Que sera sera, whatever will be will be*," but it doesn't necessarily have to be as long as you take every step to mitigate it. Fast, flexible, fearless business thinking is the only way forward.

* *

The fearlessness factor #forgetstrategy

@GETRESULTSBOOK

Fear is not a "real" thing. It does not exist until we create it

The only place it can exist is in our thoughts about the future. We do not fear the past

Fear is a product of our imagination: it creates scenarios in our mind causing us to fear things that do not presently, and may never, exist

Danger is real, but fear is a choice

We are all telling ourselves a story. We can change the story so we can eliminate the fear

Once fear is eliminated, greatness can occur

"Don't be afraid to take a big step if one is required. You cannot cross a chasm in two jumps."

David Lloyd George

2
FREEDOM

"I believe people should be given the freedom to act and think independently. With freedom comes responsibility."

The Problem: *Heading into unknown territory*

In the spring of 2013 Telecity acquired a new data centre, in Istanbul – Turkey was a completely fresh territory for us – and I needed to make the deal happen fast. However, Rob, who had successfully handled the majority of acquisitions for us in the previous years, had just moved over to head up our UK operation. He volunteered to help with the Istanbul deal but I didn't want to pluck him out of that key role so soon after he had started in his new position and, in any case, I wanted him to concentrate on the new job.

The deal was important and difficult – a major acquisition in a new market – but I didn't have time to go through the process of recruiting a replacement for Rob. I needed to deploy the resources currently available among the management team, and that was going to mean asking two of my core team to take on something they had never done before in their lives. But that's how you learn. On the job. On the edge.

The Solution: *Pushing the boundaries*

I decided to give the task to Matthew, my head of Investor Relations, and James, who runs Telecity's communications and marketing. Although both of them had been actively involved in previous acquisitions, this would be the first time they were leading the whole operation. Matthew was a city boy (though an entirely delightful one) who had previously worked at Gallaher Group, Citi and Merrill Lynch. Before joining us, James had worked in senior positions in marketing and communications for companies in Italy and the UK. They were both colleagues I trusted completely, who had enormous talents and experience; but in these particular tasks they were as yet untested.

However, in my heart, I knew they had capability to do the job brilliantly, as long as I allowed them the freedom to continue developing their existing abilities, and if I gave them the confidence to make the most of that freedom. Matthew would lead the negotiations and close the deal, James would run the post-deal integration.

When I briefed them, knowing that I was asking a lot of them and that they might be a little apprehensive, I said, "Listen, you are an extension of me. You completely understand what the ethos of our company is. We have been working together long enough for you to know the values of this company as well as, if not even better than me. We have decided this is the deal we want to do. I will give you a maximum price. You negotiate the hell out of that, do the best deal you can, and for all the other elements, you know best because you know them. Intuitively you know."

The Outcome: *A team for the future*

Matthew and James immediately got stuck in and went over to Istanbul. There they struck the great deal that I had asked for. The way that they both grew as human beings was truly out-standing. As further acquisitions came on the horizon, I now had a team in place that was a unique asset to the company, with people who could lead the way on the acquisitions and, in turn, impart their new knowledge, experience and confidence.

Later, Matthew recognized that it had been a brave move. At the beginning he had felt a little daunted but, by taking on the challenge and the responsibility, as well as knowing that I did not need to hear about every little detail – I just wanted him and James to make it happen – he had found the process empowering.

Once the deal was in place, there was a further opportunity for me to create a sense of freedom and responsibility. Selçuk, the owner of the data centre in Istanbul, had started the company up in his bedroom, and then built it up to be the market leader in Turkey. He was a young guy, quite shy, introverted, a bit of a technical geek to be honest. He and his wife were expecting a baby, and he had just received a very large sum of money as part of the acquisition. I asked Selçuk to stay on and run the business for me. With the same passion, and the same intensity. He said, "But my life has changed. I don't have to work again."

So I introduced Selçuk to the team, got him involved in the spirit and the vision and then asked Maurice, who is our country manager in Ireland, to get involved. Maurice had been through a comparable situation, when we had bought his business in Ireland two years before. He had stayed on and proved to be brilliant, really enjoying the role. So I arranged for him to mentor Selçuk, to go to Istanbul every two weeks and talk him through their similar experiences, what to expect, what he was likely to feel.

I did not brief Maurice. I gave him the freedom to handle the mentoring his way. As first, when I asked him to go and spend some time with this guy, he said, "Why would I want to do that, Mike? I am running Ireland." "Just go and have a chat with him." The reason I did not give him a specific brief was because I knew, again, that we thought in the same way, and that he would be able to impart the message immediately. It did not have to be embellished. And thanks to Maurice we were able to persuade Selçuk to stay on as the country manager for the business we had just acquired.

* *

Freedom in business comes in many forms. Each one of them – used in the right spirit – has the power to liberate you. From those freedoms you can rid yourself of whatever is preventing you from becoming free to succeed. These are my Four Freedoms for Business.

1 The freedom to have a vision

People often don't believe me when I say things. Like when I talk about the swimming with sharks experience, and everyone thinks I have made it up.

Outsiders, journalists, business experts and advisers don't believe that I run my business with a vision.

They don't believe that I have no strategy. And yet I stand up there and say "I don't believe in strategy, only vision." During the IPO – the Initial Public Offering – for TelecityGroup our advisers constantly told me, "Don't you dare say that in front of the investors because the share price is going to hit the floor. The investors want strategy."

My view was this: the investors want to believe in something, yes, they want to be convinced, but what are they actually buying into? How much of my share price value on day one, when we IPO, is going to be based on the story over the next five years and how much is going to be on my track record?

"Well," the advisers said, "you have no track record as a public company." Of course. "So what do you expect to happen to my share price from IPO?" "It is going to go down." And what happened to our share price? Sure enough, boom, it went down, for a year after we IPO'd. Then, once we had developed some track record, it started to go back up – and up. Trust me I'm a doctor, trust me I'm a doctor, trust me I'm a doctor . . . When I stood there and said, "I have no strategy" – shock horror for the future. *It would have gone down anyway . . .*

Having a vision rather than a strategy is incredibly liberating. The freedom it provides allows you to empower, inspire and adapt to changing situations. But it goes against all the received wisdom of how business should be approached, of how companies should be run. If you have the faith to trust your vision then, when you succeed, not only you but everyone around you will understand that there is another way to view the world.

2 The freedom to do things differently

When I am with my kids, one of my daughters will be over here doing this, my other daughter is asking me a question, my son is trying to attract my attention. And I am guilty of this as much as anybody else: I'll say, "Stop, stop – just let me deal with one thing at a time."

And then I sit there and think, "Now, when do I ever deal with one thing at a time in the office? I am dealing with multiple things. And yet I don't do it when I am at home." I seem to have a different tolerance level, a different capacity at home. Now clearly those are not my boundaries of capacity, because I outperform those boundaries at the office, so I am self-imposing those.

This is the issue of conscious incompetence *[see page 216]*. It comes to the fore dealing with kids because your frustration levels go right through the roof. It is unnecessary because you would never react like that in the office. There is so much more that can be achieved by taking our office performance home, than there is trying to separate the two and run them differently.

I am not advocating that you should treat your home life like a business process, but if you truly intertwine them then you should not have much of a distinction between having fun, enjoying quality of life, making important decisions, having integrity, being honest, showing empathy and tolerance. I don't see why it should differ.

For me there is no clear division between work and home – it is all my life. If I look back through the list of guests who we invited to our wedding in 2012 there are very few friends who were not involved with me through business of some sort, either in the past or currently. My wife, Shalina, and I – whose friends are mine and vice versa – act as a catalyst because we brought those people together to interact with other people.

At home I apply the principles I subscribe to at work. Sometimes it is hard to do, but I use my very best endeavours. I think that is important.

> *"There is no material difference between the way I lead my company and the way I lead my life."*

Recalibrating the work–life balance gives you the freedom to do things differently, to think about ways of doing business differently, not meekly following the same old, same old.

For example, a business colleague once said to me, "Mike, you have 15 direct reports, that can't be sustainable." "Why not?" "Well, best practice says that you should only have 7 or 8 direct reports."

"Best practice?" I said "Give me ten publicly listed companies on the FTSE 100 who follow this best practice and I will show you we have outperformed every one of them over the past five years, guaranteed. I don't care who you bring up because there is only one other company that has outperformed us over five years and I know how they operate."

"Best practice" is essentially a cop out. This is the whole point about strategy again. Have a vision. It doesn't matter the way we change our operation. The way we operate can be evolving. In most instances if you think about doing something for five years, you will be overtaken by someone who is actually doing it.

At Telecity we are, by doing what we do, creating best practice; but when we create it we would not necessarily advocate someone else doing it our way, because they should do what works best for them. This is about subverting and inverting preconceptions and prejudgments based on past information. Who would have assumed that all these companies on the internet who were giving free services would now have multi-million dollar values like Google – it's a search engine: how do you make money out of a search engine? Not the way we made money out of other products. They understood – intuitively or deliberately – the freedom to be different.

There is a lovely song called "Cat's In The Cradle" by Harry Chapin. It tells the story of a kid who has been given a new football for his birthday. He wants to play with his dad, but his dad says, "I'm busy with work, I have got something on, but don't worry because as soon as I have done this, then we will have a good time together." The kid says, "That's OK" and turns away, with a smile, and thinking "One day, I'm going to be like you, Dad." He still believes in his father.

In the next verse the son asks his father to help him with his homework. "I can't, I've got this important thing to do, but don't worry, I will help you soon." And so it goes on. Years pass, and the dad phones up his son. "Hey son, how are you doing? It's been a while since you came round and visited me. I don't see you, what's the deal?" The son says, "Well, you know how it is, dad, I'm busy with the kids, business is hectic, but don't worry, we will come and visit soon . . ." The son has become his father. In its own way, that is the pattern of "best practice."

3 The freedom that technology offers

My life is a mobile life. I am completely self-sufficient on my iPhone. Wherever I am, I can book flights on my BA app, search hotel apps for accommodation, order food from my Tesco app, bet on the football with my Betfair app. I can order a cab with Addison Lee or Hailo. I have immediate access to my bank account, stock market quotes and the performance of Telecity-Group. If I see a product I like I can use my barcode reader and scan it in.

If I am on a business trip I can check the weather in the location I am heading for so I can pack the right mix of clothes. When I get to the airport the boarding pass is on the phone. Everything I need to know for my trip is on my phone (automatically backed up, because you don't want to lose your phone and the substance of your life in one go . . .).

If I have an emotional reaction to a place, a person, a painting, I can take an image, improve it, adjust it, upload it to a site, send it to friends.

If I have a thought in the middle of the night – and those are very often the very best thoughts, business-changing thoughts – I reach for my smartphone, put the idea into it, send myself a text and then I have released the idea to the technology. My mind is freed up. I can go back to sleep.

Everything is at my fingertips. Context is king – not content. IT consumers have to have content when and where they want it; otherwise it is useless. Soon this information will be ever-there, all around us on screens – in taxi cabs or on city walls – allowing us to access personal information through finger-print recognition. You won't even need the mobile phone.

"I don't have a PA or a secretary. Nobody on my team does. But we do have the latest gadgetry."

Technology is now ubiquitous.

This I find enormously liberating, which plays into a personal fear of mine: a fear of lack of control. I really do not like to delegate a significant part of my life. I am happy to delegate within the business – as you'll see from the story at the start of this chapter, I think it is vital – but in terms of, say, booking flights or hotels, I want to do it myself. And technology allows me to do just that. It helps me control, more importantly to be in control of, my life. So I delegate to technology.

What I love about technology is that potential of freedom. There is of course a dark side: it can be over-complex, frustrating, even dangerous – we all know about those dangers – but like any inanimate part of our lives, it is the people who use technology who make it dangerous. Guns and knives by themselves do not have the power to hurt people.

There is still a surprising lack of trust in technology. Surprising because the truth is that there is no alternative.

Consider some of these realities:

- The exponential growth in the impact of technology will continue to radically transform the way we live and work. Stay at the cutting edge, not behind the blade.

- US government estimates indicate that anyone studying now will have had 10 to 14 jobs by the age of 38. The job for life has gone forever. In business we have to recognize this knowledge shift now.

- Technology has become an indispensable tool in the education of today's students: they think in different ways – Generation Net. If we don't embrace this generation, they will slip through our fingers.

And yet, there persists a stubborn, Luddite belief that we can manage without engaging with the changes happening every day. But the truth is that the clock will not be turned back.

It is great at one level that there has been a revival of vinyl records – but that is all to do with the acoustics involved. It does not actually signal a reversal of progress. Think about the 1.1 billion users on Facebook. That is a trend that is not going to be kicked. So there is no advantage in fighting technology. It is an unnecessary waste of energy in a battle that can't be won.

"I do not fear computers. I fear the lack of them."

Isaac Asimov

This is the time to ride the wave of change without being dragged under by the weight of old-school thinking. In the most brutal of terms: it's this way or no way.

Embrace technology. Enhance efficiency. Emancipate yourself.

4 The freedom to trust your instincts – and your staff

I work in the technology sector, in an IT business that is based around serious, high-level hardware and software. So you'd probably imagine that yes, of course, I make the most of all the available technology, the latest bits of kit. It comes with the territory. And that is true to a certain degree.

But there is one significant area where I do not want to enjoy, exploit or deploy technology. And that is my instinct. All the gizmos and the gadgets are there to free up my gut feeling.

As a company we took a conscious decision not to use video-conferencing for certain elements of the business. This runs counter to current thinking: conferencing is the green option, the carbon footprint is minimal. But the way I work is by running my company on trust, on emotion. I don't believe in running it on data, only verifying my decisions with data. I can get any analyst to tell me what I want to hear with the same available data.

So, I am a contradiction. I use online services religiously, deliberately to avoid human interaction, but when I do business I want to experience that gut feeling, and I go to the person, go back to the basics. If I am going to invest £100 million in a new data centre, or a new acquisition, I want to have the opportunity to look deep into the other person's eyes, read their body language. I will get on a plane and go and see them.

As well as trusting your own instincts, you have to trust – genuinely – the instincts of your staff. As every year passes, another cycle of Generation Net arrives in the workplace. This is creating a pressing business problem: how to manage people with hypertext scatterbrains. To do that you need to create knowledge space around values, articulate those values and your vision, and then rely on people to manage themselves.

Learn to work in tandem with your younger staff: those hypertext minds think in a completely different way, which you will need to understand and relate to. *[See Chapter 8 Focus]* Allow your staff to manage their own time and they will be on call for you 24/7. And it might also help with the kids at home . . .

How people react to freedom differs. In the book *Who Moved My Cheese?*, Spencer Johnson tells the story of two mice who go to the same place for their cheese. Someone takes the cheese away and moves it to another place. One mouse sits there, miserable, thinking "Oh no, no cheese." The other one realizes, "What is for sure is I am not going to get anything to eat if I sit here moping about it. I need to think *not* that there is no cheese left but that perhaps someone has moved it, and it might be as easy to find as it was the first time." Sitting there you are going to die.

You can start observing types of people, and learn how to spot a reaction process in someone before they do it. If this is going to happen, you know that they are going to react in this way, and therefore maybe you can help him or her along a different path.

We all have different freedoms

Within the staff of a company, and in the people you meet and do business with, the perception of what "freedom" means varies enormously. You need to be aware that it will often differ from your own, and that you need to be empathetic to those variances. Your antennae need to be attuned.

For some younger staff, their aim is to come to the job, work hard, get paid and go out at the weekend for a release, to have some fun, have a hangover on Sunday morning and know they are coming back to work on Monday. They do not have liabilities or family dependents, so the fact that they can go home at the end of the evening and relax – unless there is a call to action stations for an emergency – means that they are not worrying. That is their freedom. Providing security, structure and rules can reinforce a sense of freedom.

Whereas I expect unusual and disproportionate slices of my management team's mindset – and of their lives, at certain times – and as a result I need to give them a different kind of freedom, to enable their ability to deliver that. If they have family commitments, I need to be mindful of that. By giving them the freedom to do all the things they need as part of their grown-up lives, they become more valuable to me, because it frees their mind to focus on the things I would like them to focus on.

I have learnt to try to identify what freedom means to other people. When I was at Redbus, we were going through a round of quite extreme cost- and staff-cutting, with no money in the pipeline. It was survival mode. One of the team, Dave, was critical because he was one of the few people left who had the infrastructure knowledge of our buildings. At the time, Heathrow Terminal 5 was being built, and other major construction projects were underway, so the infrastructure skills he had were in huge demand.

In my mind I was thinking that I could not afford to pay him much more money than he was getting currently, and that all the other infrastructure specialists were being tempted away to other companies, especially as they thought Redbus was about to go bust.

So I sat down with Dave, and said, "I am in a pickle here as your boss. I can't afford what I fear you are going to want, but I really don't want you to leave. You are important to me." He said, "Mike, this may surprise you. Although more money would make a difference – and the more money you give me the happier I will be – what is more important to me is getting to see my kids every couple of weeks." He had been through a divorce and his children lived with their mother in Wales. Every fortnight he fought his way out of London to drive all the way down to Wales, was shattered on a Saturday morning and then had to leave at midday on the Sunday for the long haul back to London.

He asked if he could have ten or fifteen days' additional holiday each year so that he could take a Friday off, travel down early, and spend more time with the children. I knew he was good for it. He would do all the hard work I needed in the other four days of the week.

Allowing him to formally take an extra day off every few weeks was what kept him in the company, not the salary. Understanding that freedom was the key. So all my concerns about not being able to pay him enough, that he was going to follow his mates out of the door, none of the worry was applicable. I could have cut out all of that by proactively going up to him much

earlier and saying, "Let's talk about what is important to you."
A lesson learnt.

*   *

Remember, be free to have a vision. Don't assume you can't do
something just because it is far away or because it is improba-
ble, or even seemingly impossible. A thousand years ago, could
we have envisaged flying to New York in three hours by Concorde? "Sorry what's Concorde? . . . three hours to America? I
can't even get to the end of the road in three hours. Londinium
is more than three hours away!"

*"Probability and possibility are only defined by our own
boundaries. Not by the world we live in."*

If you follow that mindset, it means that almost never in life is
a single minute not important to you. Even when you are sleeping it is valuable because it makes you alert and receptive to the
next day's challenge.

Feeling and believing a vision is the first step to it becoming a
reality. And then feel that you are exploiting every second. It is
a habit-forming thing. I really believe that I can't be doing anything better or more valuable to me than what I am doing right
now. If you have to ask yourself, "Well, is it?" that in itself drives
you to being more fruitful.

Sometimes I sit down, phew, I need a break. And I'll play a FIFA
football game for five minutes. Now, is that a waste of time? No,

because it is resetting my mind. It is getting me out of something I am into too deep. Then I can move on. I don't even finish the game, done. Every second is useful even if you think it is wasting time.

There's an expression "Time is money." Think of it this way instead: Time is free. So use time to make you free. Freedom is more valuable than money!

The freedom factor #forgetstrategy

@GETRESULTSBOOK

Freedom comes at the price of responsibility. The more freedom we have, the more responsibility we take on

Release fear and increase freedom, increase freedom and increase responsibilities, increase responsibilities and limit freedom

We can create our own freedom by releasing ourselves from the mental imprisonment of fear

Freedom is a state of mind, freedom is choice

Embrace the freedom that technology offers: enhance efficiency and emancipate yourself

Think whether you can do one key thing in your life differently: change is a catalyst for liberation

---

"To be free is not merely to cast off one's chains, but to live in a way that respects and enhances the freedom of others."

Nelson Mandela

3
FLEXIBILITY

"If you make plans in concrete and worry about following them to the letter you won't be prepared for the challenges that arise – the ones you haven't even thought about."

The Problem: *Cherchez le client*

Early in my career, I found myself based in France, working for a company called Tricord Systems. We made super-servers, not that I knew what one was at the time, or had ever seen one.

The company did not yet have an office. So, one Sunday afternoon, I found myself sitting in a virtually empty flat with hardly any furniture, looking through the equivalent of the *Yellow Pages*, trying to source somebody to sell these things called super-servers to. Because, along with the lack of an office and accommodation, I was faced with a major lack of clients. It was my job to find them.

The Solution: *Let your fingers do the walking*

As I flicked through the pages trying to spot a company with an English-sounding name I came across the number for the

Paris headquarters of J. P. Morgan. Here was a company I had heard of. I thought I had half a shot at being able to talk to them in English. I dialled the number, fully expecting to find myself being bounced around the internal phone system before I could get the name of anyone who might have the power to make a buying decision. As it happened, the person who picked up the phone turned out to be an American, a vice president in charge of their IT infrastructure, who had come in to the office over the weekend to catch up on work. A complete fluke.

We ended up having a robust discussion – just this side of a full-on argument – with him telling me there was no way he wanted to talk to me. I had to keep thinking on my feet, constantly adapting and adjusting my line of attack, responding to every counterargument he threw at me until he agreed to an appointment, probably just to get me off the phone.

The Outcome: *La vie en rose*

By the time I arrived for the meeting with the vice president at J. P. Morgan, Ralph Ziegler, he had taken the time to research Tricord Systems and revealed that his company was looking to buy super-servers in the near future. He bought them from me. It turned out to be a very lucrative deal. J. P. Morgan became a very significant client – not only did that demonstrate to my new bosses that I could deliver serious clients, but in turn that became a reference point for my next round of sales calls. When

I was asked who else had bought one of these super-servers I could say, "J. P. Morgan bought some only last week."

The J. P. Morgan offices are based in the Place Vendôme, also home to the Hôtel Ritz. Underneath the square is a maze of tunnels with vaults containing safes and deposit boxes. Ralph took me down there to show me the vaults and we became good friends.

We had an affinity, because he was an English speaker in Paris just as I was. When we had first spoken on the phone that Sunday afternoon, and he was being quite brusque and brash with me – "You'll never get a meeting with me, calling me at this unholy time" – I had been able to respond, turning it into a joke in a way that I think no French salesperson, even a fluent English speaker, could not have done. You would think that not being French and trying to sell computers there would have put me at a disadvantage, but in fact the opposite had been the case.

I learnt many other lessons about flexibility during my time in France.

When I first arrived in Paris to work for another French company, Goupil, I spent the first few days urgently trying to organize an apartment for myself. This was not an easy task: rental property in Paris was at a premium and it was a landlord's market. My knowledge of French was somewhere between pretty minimal and non-existent. Oh, and it was a weekend. French estate agents didn't work at weekends . . . With a mixture of chutzpah and hustle I found an apartment by the Monday morning.

Later, I was looking for a different job. I picked up the newspaper and noticed an advert – in English – recruiting a PA for the CEO of a start-up operation called ICG, International Computer Group. I called them and said I didn't want to be a PA, but if they were just starting up there must be a role for me. The CEO, Gareth Cadwallader, had only recently arrived in Paris, and the team was just him; I could relate to that. He invited me along for a meeting, I joined the company and worked there for four years.

*   *

Vision is flexible. Strategy is static.

This comes back to the issue of vision and strategy. Vision is eminently, infinitely flexible. Strategy – especially in a business, corporate environment – is by its very nature not flexible.

Strategy has to be written down, and it is impossible to write for every single eventuality. You can try. You can get an entire team working on a strategy document, setting out every conceivable option and element. And then something changes that no one had considered, and if you live by strategy you are stuck.

But if you have got a vision it doesn't matter what happens, because you will know how to adapt your answer to whatever happens because you only have to refer to the shared vision. Think of it in these terms: forget the map, but bring a compass.

Let me give you an example.

In 2013 there was a huge fire in the building next door to our Paris operation, a serious blaze that destroyed the other building and threatened to force every business nearby to shut down operations.

The firefighters came in to see our staff and said they had to leave immediately even though there was no direct personal threat to them. Our fire engines, *les pompiers* explained, will be blocking all your exits, and we will probably be here for at least all of today, maybe even longer. Even though it would have been easier to pack up and go, my staff said, "Fine, we are happy for you to lock us in." They selected a core team of six people, evacuated the rest of the personnel, and stayed there for as long as it took for the fire to be conquered, making sure that the company could keep operating and continue servicing our customers and clients.

Which is why I get quite exercised about the whole rigmarole – the restrictions of corporate governance, values, ethics. Because you cannot legislate for what happened in Paris. What could I put into an employee handbook to tell the staff that their loyalty to the customer base must be so strong that they should stay put even in the event of a fire? The legislators would hit you for health and safety, anyway. But, more importantly, I don't want the staff to feel obliged – even if they don't want to

– to stay in the building simply because it is a procedure that is written into some strategy document. I want them to make that decision for themselves, by themselves, and only because they really want to. The reason they want to is because they have subscribed to a vision which is strong enough and flexible enough to respond to any given situation that might crop up. (Thank you to Stéphane, my French MD.)

It has got to be in their minds constantly. It has got to be in their hearts. That is an important part of the way we operate the business.

> *"By actively encouraging a shared vision, the long-term sustainability of a business is also encouraged."*

I was attending a conference in Boston, and had a meeting with some investors. One of them had been an investor since the company's IPO in 2007, and had shared in the significant stock increase across the years. Alongside him was a potential investor, who was considering whether to come in or not. He was saying, "OK Mike, I get it. I understand. And I regret not buying the stock earlier, but I am going to take the plunge. But I have one question. You are synonymous with Telecity. Telecity and Michael Tobin are linked; you can't separate them. So what happens if you get hit by a bus?"

And before I could answer, the investor who had been there since 2007 turned to him, and said, "A cheese sandwich could run this business."

What? "A cheese sandwich could run this business." Then I got what he was saying. The point he was making was that a) I was not interdependent with the business, b) our delivery was consistent, and c) in these very insecure times when markets are so volatile, the business model is as simple and as stable as a cheese sandwich. I took it as a compliment.

I am at the heart of the vision, but the vision is not dependent on me. It has a life and a vitality beyond me. I was not in Paris when the fire broke out and I didn't discuss the staff's decision to stay with them. TelecityGroup can survive without me because it will retain the vision.

Doing nothing is never a solution

Flexibility allows you to make the difficult decisions. It is very easy to get locked into the "difficulty" of the decision. That is when you need to break out of that way of viewing decisions.

No-brainers are called that because they do not require you to use any brain time. If the decision is obvious, make it.

The same people who would subscribe to that attitude then turn around and say they can't make their mind up: between this decision or that decision, this choice or that choice.

My take on that is that if the two choices are that close, then whichever decision you make can't be that bad. One might be marginally less good than the other but the differential is going to be pretty minimal. Toss a coin and call it.

The worst thing to do is not to make a decision.

I once found myself in that position when I was "umming and aahing" over whether to change a key staff member. I was coming up with a whole range of reasons why I could put off a decision that, in my heart, I knew I ought to make. I was weighing up the decision against the potential impact on the company.

It took someone from outside to make me see the problem. "If you don't make this change, Mike, what you are saying is that the reasons that you are not doing it have become your problem now. Remember, you are making the call. If this was your business and it wasn't a public company what would you do?" I said, "I'd ask them to leave, instantly." "OK, then that's your call."

When I talk about business issues with my people it helps me to walk through a scenario, helps me to think about it in my own way as well. By listening to myself talk, without them necessarily suggesting things, I am helping to clarify the issues within my mind. Another example of staying flexible.

Flexibility should be a mindset for all staff from top down, including the skill of listening to views from throughout the organization.

"The reasonable man adapts himself to the world. The unreasonable man persists in trying to adapt the world to him . . . All progress therefore depends upon the unreasonable man."

George Bernard Shaw

Give decisions maximum flexibility

The other element of retaining flexibility in decision-making is to leave the final decision as late as possible. My deadline for pressing buttons is right at the very last moment, no earlier. Then, regardless of anything beyond, I have made my decision – and, even if it proves to be wrong, if it was that close, the decision is still going to be as good as it can be. That is your deadline.

Wait for the last possible moment to decide, because so many things may change in the meantime. The internet is exaggerating that point because it provides a constant flow of information, which is updating and changing all the time.

If you are on a path towards a decision, you will probably set out a series of steps you need to make to get to the decision point. Don't be tempted to go any earlier – you may get more information close to the deadline that will alter what that decision should be. Always start with the deadline for the decision and work backwards.

Love it, leave it, change it

With business problems it is not unusual to get bogged down in the problem, to allow it to become so all-consuming that it blinkers you from the path ahead.

There is a mantra I believe in completely: Love it, leave it, change it.

This was something I learnt from the yogi Jagdish Parikh. He once told me that if anything is troubling you, if you don't like anything in your life, whatever it is, if you are unhappy in a marriage or a job, there are only three actions that can improve it.

Doing nothing – not making a decision, or carrying on with the status quo – is not the answer. You will be permanently unhappy and you will be wasting and ruining your life with unhappiness, as well as (most likely) the lives of other people. So you have three options: love it, leave it or change it.

Love it: you have got to truly love what is currently making you unhappy. And that is a very hard thing to do. But, if you can get your mind not to fake it, to truly learn to love it, then your problem has gone.

Accept it as it truly is, on a mental level. If you have lost someone you love, accept it. There are plenty of strategies available on how you can do that, but once you have accepted it, it doesn't have the power to hurt you any more.

Leave it: just walk away, and then your problem has gone. You may have other problems, but that problem has gone.

Leave it, walk away from the pain. That is not so easy as losing someone, because you can't walk away from having lost them, they have already gone. If you are with someone who is not making you happy, learn to like what they are doing that currently does not make you happy, or try to change them, try to stop them doing the things that don't make you happy.

But you have the option of walking away.

Change it: try to change what is in front of you and making you unhappy.

If you are not doing one of those three things, what might seem like the fourth option – of doing nothing – is not in fact an option, because it is an insult to your own life, and to the parents who invested so much into your birth and upbringing.

Most people go for the option of change; they try to change the situation. OK, how do you change? Most things can be changed to an extent, but if it can't be changed, if it *truly* can't be changed, then why are you feeling stressed about it, because you go back to square one again: love it or leave it. If you can change it, it doesn't matter what it is you do as long as there is progress. Whatever you can do, do.

This is difficult to put into practice. Many times when I have tried to apply this to my own life, I have rarely got it right, and I have ended up for a long time stuck in that virtual option 4, sitting there stagnating.

You may think I think I am clever being able to write about these things but, believe me, there are so many situations in my life where I struggle with this one principle of "Love it, leave it or change it." It is possibly the most powerful, the most simple and yet the most difficult piece of advice to follow.

It's a natural human reaction. Nobody likes change. We only like change when we are in control of the change. So if we have the lever we are happy to be in control. If we are driving recklessly in a car we are happy because it's fun, but if we are a passenger and someone else is driving recklessly we are panicking because we are not in control of what is going on.

We don't like change unless we are the instigators of it, and when change happens outside our control we are generally not comfortable. Status quo is our default.

I aim to pass on the "Love it, leave it, change it" philosophy through the company. Inevitably, if staff are unhappy at home it is going to affect their performance at work. One of the useful things I do in the face-to-face meetings with my country managers is to listen to them talk about stuff from home. All I am doing is listening. Because I can't help them in their marriage or other personal situation, but I can listen. That gives them an audience, someone to empathize with them, which often calms them down and allows them to concentrate on the issues to do with the business and the company.

Small businesses and start-ups are always flexible: retain and foster that ability to respond to change as companies expand

Business in a joined-up world requires flexibility. On a typical morning recently I had four phone calls, about M&A deals, while I was walking from Elephant & Castle to Westminster to take part in a debate about education. From there, heading back to the office, I chaired another conference call in the cab. As soon as I was in the office I had a call with the CEO of a major telco trying to resolve a difficult, and potentially litigious, personnel issue.

On my to-do list for the rest of the day I was trying to buy a business in Ireland – we had an offer out and were haggling about pricing. We were negotiating to buy a business in Italy at the same time, at a slightly different stage of the process, positioning ourselves with their management team, as well as looking at companies in Eastern Europe. A conversation had just started up with a Polish business. On the other hand I was trying to understand who might want to buy us, with our share price shooting up, and wondering if a rumour was driving it. I had seen 68 investors over the previous three weeks including three trips to the US. I had a Swedish company board meeting to close the annual accounts in the evening, and an Irish board meeting. I was seeing a headhunter to fill a major role within the company, and entertaining business guests in the evening.

There are always a million things going on. If I had a linear thought process I would have to shut down on 99% of all those different things, and I would focus on one.

I receive 300 or so emails a day and, when I get too many because I am engaged in too many other activities, I get to a point where the best thing I can do is re-send the oldest *unread* – i.e. undealt with – e-mails to myself. I take the oldest ones that I clearly haven't dealt with . . . and send them to the top of the queue. It makes the list much easier to deal with because I don't have read e-mails separating the unread ones. It gives me a motivational buzz too.

We have all started to use this technique of flexible processing, which has grown up alongside the rise of multi-platform technology. At Redbus I worked with a guy called John Porter who is the son of Dame Shirley Porter (and the grandson of Jack Cohen, the founder of the Tesco chain). John was an intriguing character. The first time I met him was in Smiths restaurant in Smithfields. He was a bit narcoleptic, so as soon as he had said, "Tell me about yourself" he fell asleep . . .

When we started working together the thing I most admired about John was his ability to jump from topic to totally disconnected topic. He was running a dozen businesses, following up other opportunities. He would be sitting there, packing a bag with his golf shoes, picking up the phone for a quick-fire, one-minute conversation, da-da-da-da, straight back in and engaged again. He was able to chop, deeply, into whatever was going on at that particular moment.

So there has to be a complete micro-slicing of life. Now that seems to me to be more like the way kids are learning today than the way they learned a hundred years ago. And if I think that is my most efficient way of operating, then that gives me a little bit of confidence that actually we are not straying away from the right thing, maybe we are closing in on the right thing.

Alongside the raft of different business activities, I have – like everybody else – all the other things in life to deal with. As I said before, I live a mobile life.

Our way of living in a web-connected world demands flexibility of mind

You can apply that to everyone who works with and for you.

As a result I don't care whether my management team is in the office today, working from home or taking an unplanned day off. I genuinely don't care. But, at 3 o'clock on a Sunday morning, if I want to talk to them I expect them to pick up the phone when I call – because if I am doing that, there is only one reason why: because it is **URGENT**. That is the way we operate. It is complete flexibility where life and work are concerned.

That is why I allow everyone to use Facebook at the office. If someone is playing a game on their computer, or doing their shopping online, that is fine. However, if I then want something, they aren't in a position to tell me they can't do it, because I know for a fact that they *have* got time. In the meantime, you are not going to tell me you can't do it, you are going to say yes. Why would I pressure you into creating structure around this free-flowing, successful enterprise?

I am happy for anyone, at whatever level in the company, to use their online banking, order their next Ocado delivery, whatever they like. Go and do what you want to do. Because work and life is so intertwined. If you expect people to work late, when are they going to have time to go to the bank? Technology makes this much easier, of course, but also creates more work.

This goes back to the point about allowing people the responsibility to be independent, giving them freedom which creates a sense of responsibility in them. That responsibility is reflected in commitment and dedication above and beyond the call of duty. It is up to them to manage their time.

I have never paid much attention to a CV in my life. The CV is less and less relevant, written to fixed structures, with meaningless personal statements copied from a common template, a regurgitation of over-hyped past achievements. What is relevant to me when I look at someone who wants to work with me and for me is, "Can I trust them and do they have the ability to evolve and be flexible?" That counts for everything. The biggest and fastest don't survive. Only the adaptable. Ask Kodak.

*   *

In 2000 I came back from Paris for a meeting with the head of ICL in Windsor. I was running really late for the meeting. The traffic out of London was terrible. I phoned up the head of HR, Peter Long, to apologize for the likely delay in my arrival and to see if we could delay the meeting. "Oh no, what a shame," he said. "We were really hoping to move the meeting forward, not back." It was not the start to an interview I had hoped for.

But when I finally got there, the CEO, David, and Peter could not have been nicer. "We were sitting here thinking how stressed you must be with all that pressure." The boss seemed to like me. He told me ICL had a company in Denmark which was in a real mess and asked me if I would be prepared to have a go at sorting it out. I took on the challenge and moved over to Copenhagen. I remembered that ability to think about what I must have been going through and the empathy they had shown. It was a humbling lesson in flexibility – demonstrated by them towards me – and it buoyed me up to take the decision to take on the challenge, which marked a significant change in my life and career.

Recently I was reminded by my head of HR of a situation where I had helped her to be flexible in her own approach. She wanted a new person for her team. At TelecityGroup we deliberately keep our level of human resources as tight as possible; there is a huge amount of expectation on everyone as a result. She was being asked by the board to achieve certain targets and she was getting some flak for not delivering one particular element. So she asked for the extra person. I said that I did not see why she needed that person. She remembers thinking that in that case she would forget it, that we should move on, and asked me to back her up at the next board meeting.

But I would not let it go. I knew there was a need but felt she was going in the wrong direction. We kept talking and, in the end, we agreed that we could expand the role of an existing member of her team rather than bringing in someone specifically for the task. She says I made her realize that she had pitched the idea in the wrong way. In that case it was my persistence in not letting the core idea go which had raised questions in her mind, which in turn led to her being flexible in her own approach and decision-making.

*　*

Flexibility at work spills over into flexibility in the rest of your life. I had completed quite a few marathons and decided I would like to take on the challenge of the London Triathlon. I had never trained for anything like it. I didn't even own a bike. However, I noticed that James, my head of Marcomms, turned up in the office every day sporting Lycra leggings and a cycling helmet, so I asked him if I could borrow his bike. He said sure, and promised that he would leave it locked up outside the office – which was close to the Triathlon start near City Airport.

I turned up early on the morning of the event and looked for his bike. It was an old-style three-speed bike, with straight handlebars, a basket and a bell, like something Mary Poppins might have ridden. I made it round the 40 kilometres . . .

Similarly, when I was waiting in the staging area in my tracksuit watching the elite performers coming in – it was an Olympic trial year. The leader came in, undoing his wetsuit. I hadn't realized I needed a wetsuit. I was planning to go out in my usual trunks. It was 9am on a foggy September morning and the swim was in the waters of the Thames. The wetsuit suddenly made a whole lot of sense. I nipped over to him. "Can I borrow your wetsuit?" "If you can get me out of the bloody thing you can!" I helped him strip it off, and watched him jump on his bike for the second stage. I popped his wetsuit on – back to front – and got ready for my mile in the waters of the Thames. I finished. Another triumph for flexible thinking . . .

The flexible factor #forgetstrategy

@GETRESULTSBOOK

Adapt or die: in the long term, it is never the strongest, the biggest or the fastest who survive, but always the most flexible

Stick to a crystal clear vision, but retain flexibility on the details

Remain obstinate about your vision but retain flexibility in the details

One of life's guarantees is that flexibility will always be more valuable than predictability

You can apply "Love it, leave it, change it" to every problem in your life in business or at home

Flexibility in thinking is perfectly in tune with the opportunities and possibilities of a web-connected world

"The measure of intelligence is the ability to change."

Albert Einstein

4
FAILURE

"I am not afraid of failure. Failure is only in the mind of the beholder. It is an attitude, not a physical state."

The Problem: *The danger of loose talk*

In the months that followed the Telecity IPO, we were taking a large number of incoming media calls. We had been the only technology IPO in the UK in the period when the world economy had dived. We had taken a huge leap of faith, little knowing that we would be the last tech IPO on the UK main market for the next four years. We kept our nerve and the IPO proved to be successful. Starved of stories about successful businesses of any kind, the press were naturally keen to sniff out information.

I called the staff together and told them: "You can't talk to the press in the same way you did when we were a private company. It doesn't matter whether it's trade press or the tabloids, a local or national paper, or whether it's an old mucker of yours from Fleet Street who 'just wants to go for a drink.' What you say *does* matter, because we are a public company. You could directly affect the share price. So when these journalists call you for a quote – as they will – you are going to have to be extra careful. 'Yeah, yeah, Mike,' they nodded, 'We are all adults, we've been fielding press calls like that for years.'"

I wasn't so confident. I had been through a number of sessions of media training and been surprised at how easy it was to be suckered. Even if you said "No comment," that in itself could be interpreted as confirming or denying the question posed.

The Solution: *Interrogation in Tallinn*

For the management meeting we went to Tallinn. I arranged for us to be picked up in four ageing Trabants, so we had to squeeze ourselves in with all our luggage for a none too comfortable ride in from the airport to the hotel. The drivers were gruff and spoke no English. In the evening we went out to an old-style restaurant, with a jolly atmosphere and local folk singing. It felt out of our time, slightly surreal, a throwback to the Soviet era.

Walking back to the hotel, down a 13th-century cobbled street, getting on for midnight, we were suddenly stopped by three armed soldiers, or police, maybe even KGB. We weren't sure, but the Kalashnikovs they were carrying looked real enough. They pushed and herded us roughly through a medieval doorway. The team looked at me. "What's going on, Mike?" I shook my head and shrugged.

We were escorted into a hallway, and one by one taken to a separate room. One of the agents took a pedestal lamp and shone it into the face of the first person. "What is your name?" he snapped. He gave his name. "Where are you from?" "London . . ." "Why are you here?" The guy muttered something about a management weekend. "Who do you work for? . . . What about your share price?" The victim babbled some information before being released.

Each member on the team went through the same routine: "Is it a good company? Should I buy shares? Are you acquiring other companies?"

By the time the fifth person had come back to the group, they had twigged what the game was, but the first four had all revealed something about our company which, if it had been relayed to a journalist, might have been sensitive to the share performance.

We finished the session and broke out some bottles of local beer. I told the team that the exercise had been organized for me by a specialist travel agency called Black Tomato, who had suggested doing something with a Soviet-era flavour. When they mentioned the KGB, it immediately triggered the thought in my mind of recreating an interrogation to address the press issue. Black Tomato had sourced the actors to play the KGB, and they did a great job.

The Outcome: *Speaking with confidence*

Over a drink we analyzed the reaction of the first few who had been interrogated. They all said that they hadn't had time to think. They had already been disorientated by being in Tallinn, then shocked and destabilized by the KGB "arrest." I told them that this time it wasn't important, because they were not journalists. But – and it was a big but – they had been coerced very easily and tricked into revealing information they should not have been talking about. They realized how easy it is to become disorientated or distracted.

James, the head of marketing and communications, was on that trip. He remembers that although he knew that the "interrogation" was not for real, that it was a game designed to make a point, even with his experience in communications he found that it was difficult to keep in his mind the sense that it was a simulation. The ten to fifteen minutes in the interrogation area seemed like a long time, and he realized how being asked direct, searching and sometimes quite personal questions could easily tempt or trick you into revealing things you would not normally have talked about openly to strangers.

The "interviewees" who had cracked were frustrated that they had failed in front of their colleagues, but I told them that was the whole point. They would never forget that "failure," and that in fact it was a success because they had helped us all appreciate how we needed to behave in the coming months and years.

Short-term failure had given us the power to change in the long term.

*   *

Since then there has been even more significant change. Now we organize regular analyst days. Every six months or so we arrange a visit for analysts, investors and the press to one of our data centres, take them on a tour round the facility, and then each of our country managers presents to the assembled audience. And I don't say a word. I let them do the talking. Sometimes I do not even attend the analyst day. That underlines the total confidence I have now, a few years down the road, to leave all of that sensitive communication to the management team.

The investors and the analysts see this as an incredibly valuable day, not least because what they are seeing in action is that the company is imbued with the vision. They have the comfort of knowing that if, heaven forbid, I get knocked down by the proverbial bus, my vision is deployed through the management. That is hugely reassuring for them. They know that we all think, eat, dream in the same way. I won't say that I am essentially surplus to requirements, but the point is made.

That all grew out of the Tallinn experience. The whole point there had been that when talking to journalists and any interested outside parties you could never be prepared. The call was always going to come when you were least expecting it, when you were flustered or distracted, or didn't even realize you were talking to a reporter.

Now being surprised should never be a surprise. It is part of life. But it happens. Through the Tallinn experience, I believe that the gut reaction of the team was altered. Before, they had been a little blasé about their media skills, instincts and nous. Afterwards, whenever they took a call, instinctively they would be thinking, "Aaah, I know what might happen". I could have told them that at training seminars for years, and during all that time the risk of somebody saying the wrong thing would still have been there. Tallinn allowed me to get that message across in one, quick, memorable hit with enduring results.

* *

Define your successes, not your failure

Failure is a vital part of business. If you only ever succeed (does anyone only ever succeed, or are they just smart at burying their failures?) then it could just be down to luck. But if you fail, and then succeed, it proves you have learnt what not to do.

I know this for a fact because over the course of my life there have been many occasions when I haven't got things totally right. The litany of failures that litter my past is evidence that I continually get it wrong. (But that's for the next book . . .)

First you have to define what success means to you. Don't let yourself be influenced by what other people think – they will probably have different views, and it is irrelevant if you don't achieve success in someone else's eyes. It is about you delivering what you personally believe to be your success criteria. If you achieve that, anything beyond is an upside.

Ask the question: what is success? If you toss a coin, and you call heads or tails, you are either going to be 100% successful or you will be a 100% failure. But life isn't about calling heads or tails. Success can be defined as a variable: yes, clearly there is failure, and clearly there is success but, in between, is an area with a myriad of nuances and countless shades of grey.

As you move towards success you can relativize it. You can say to yourself, "I have been successful in this and that but I didn't quite manage to achieve this." For instance, when I was 16 I decided that I wanted to be a millionaire by 18. When I was 18 I hadn't made it, so I said, "Right. I am going to be a millionaire by 21." When I reached 21, it was definitely going to be 25 and, at 25, I pushed the target back to 30.

Priorities change, and eventually you may reach a point where certain targets are of no consequence any more. Now, I don't even think of becoming a millionaire as success but, over so much of my early life, my early working life, I "failed." I did not achieve my own objectives. In the context of where I am today it is irrelevant, but it did not seem like it at the time.

All these things are relative: relative to time, relative to our experience and relative to our ability to project our own worth.

If you think about how happy you are, or how unhappy you are, then you can affect your ability to be successful. So if "successful" is only defined by yourself, for example, then by changing your mood you become instantly more successful regardless of any outcome. Simply by changing your view of what you did, rather than what you actually did.

I can make you more successful in one easy statement: think higher of yourself and you will be more successful in your own eyes. As we have just defined it, success is only a relative thing in the view of the people beholding it. So we can all become a whole nation of very successful people instantly.

Consider the saying, "Shoot for the moon, because even if you miss it you will land among the stars." By definition of that statement you failed because you didn't get the moon. But how bad is it?

I was recently reading about the concept of being able to do anything. That is a throwaway statement; everyone in business talks about motivation: "You can do anything you want to do." But in reality you can't do anything. I can't be an astronaut tomorrow, for instance, can I? But the question can be thrown back at you.

Someone can ask you, "Well, did you phone up NASA and ask them if you could be an astronaut?" "Of course not, because I assume I can't be" – and that is your first failing point. Saying you can do anything may be a throwaway statement, but it is a placeholder for a process in life that refuses to accept mediocrity or your current self.

In other words, "I want to be an astronaut," yes, it most likely is not going to happen, but have you done everything in your power to try to make it happen? Everything I have done in my life, I would have said I wouldn't have been able to do it, until I did it, and I only did it because I took a step towards it. You don't know what happens after you take that first step; the road changes.

If you are really going to encourage people to go out of their comfort zone to such an extreme that they are more likely to fail than not because of the super-stretch targets they have given themselves, then actually you need to reward for failure.

In the company we use the word "success." We don't necessarily use the word "failure" just because we don't achieve some of the things we set out to do. As long as you fail on the way towards those targets, it is only about the relative distance that you are from where your – possibly outrageous – aspirations were in the first place.

Because how bad can failure be? We are all consumed by the fear of failing when actually failing is only our own opinion of not achieving what we internally set out to do. Looking from the outside someone could have seen us as incredibly success-ful. One person's failure is somebody else's success.

Be honest with yourself and others about what you consider your failures to be and both you, and they, will value your achievements much more. Yogi Berra, the legendary New York Yankees catcher and manager, understood the positive value of failure. "Losing is a learning experience," he once said. "It teaches you humility. It teaches you to work harder."

That is why I always prefer to see job candidates who are pre-pared to reveal setbacks and failures they have encountered in previous jobs, and how they were able to improve their performance as a result, rather than applicants who have remarkably airbrushed seamless careers – simply because I never believe they are genuine.

One of the questions candidates are often asked at the end of a job interview is, "If you could say something bad about yourself what would it be?" Or "Is there something you wish you had done and haven't?" That is because they are trying to prise out something that is not as glossy as you portrayed. Of course everyone has to sell themselves, so you are selling yourself on your best game. But life is life.

When I recruit, the key question I have in my mind is not about whether they can do the job or have the skill set that they are telling me about. If I click with them, and there is a chemistry, if I sense that the person in front of me is going to be able to do remarkable things, I am asking myself, "Are they happy to make mistakes and progress rapidly?" Mistakes just prove that you are doing something. It is guaranteed that if you do nothing, you probably won't make any mistakes. Making repeated mistakes for an illogical reason is Einstein's definition of insanity: "Doing the same thing over and over again and expecting different results." A mistake, a failure, is not bad in itself. The inability to learn from those mistakes and failures, on the other hand . . .

"Fear of failure closes you up. Feeling you have the power to change, to do something, is powerful. Don't worry about mistakes."

"No" is a journey towards "yes"

When I started out as a salesman, I was taught this lesson – by Bryan Adams' cousin Ian Watson, as it happened – how to look at the cold call, where someone slams the door in your face, or hangs up on you, as a positive step towards success. Let's assume you win one deal in every three that you make an offer for; that you get asked to make an offer for one in every ten clients who have an interest; and that you find a prospect who has an interest in every 20 cold calls you place.

That means, on average, one sale for every 600 cold calls you make. In other words, every "No," every failure is actually

1/600th of a "Yes." The message was: get out there and start getting your "no's."

I always approach things with the attitude of putting the target out there and walking backwards from that. "What is the last thing that happened before you achieved that target?" "I signed this deal." "With whom, by the way? How did you identify that person?" "Well, it was one of these three."

"Ah, now we have three targets, not just one. These three targets, where did you get them?" "I probably found them from a list of phone calls that I made." "OK, now we've got a list of phone calls, let's say 60 phone calls. Where did you get those numbers from?" Work back and back and back.

That objective is broken down into a thousand objectives, of which many will fail. To be successful you had to sign that deal and to get that deal you needed three deals on the go, two of which you knew would fail. In order to get three deals on the boil, you probably needed 50 deals to be on the go. In order to have 50 opportunities to send an offer out to, you probably needed to call 1000 people, so clearly to get one deal, you have 999 failures – *if* you look at them as failures.

Again, it is about relativizing the meaning of failure and success. Like high jumping. High jumping is a really weird sport because you only win when you fail. In virtually every other athletic sport – apart from pole vaulting – you finish first, you're ahead of everyone else, it's a clear result. In long jump it is simple:

who jumps furthest. But with the high jump you keep going until you actually fail. And then you say, the one before I failed is my height.

It is an unusual way of defining who is best since everyone fails at the end. It is just that your previous success was better than everyone else's, but you still ultimately fail. In a controlled environment like that you know you're not going to upset anyone by failing once you've broken the world record: if you fail the next time, who cares?

You go to the point of your own failure to demonstrate how good you are. It is a shame that life is not about going to the point of your own failure to demonstrate how good you are.

But if you're in business, doing one deal after another, and you just happen to be good at these deals but you are pushing and pushing and pushing, and suddenly you do a bad deal, your reputation is impacted. You can do a thousand good things to build a reputation and just one bad thing and it's gone.

That is a major difference between the US and the UK. If you succeed in the US you are great, if you succeed in the UK, you are great. Fine. But if you fail in the UK, you are a disaster, hopeless, game over. Whereas in the US you are still great, because they say, "Well, he's not going to do that again, is he? That is part of the learning curve." It is a different way of looking at failure: it is an asset to you, of value to you.

Fail at the hurdles, win at the goals

The whole concept I have of failure is: first of all I don't do "normal," so if I am not doing something normal, I am doing something *ab*normal. From my point of view if I am doing something that has never been done before, if I am testing the waters, or pushing the edge of the boundary, I am by definition going to fail sometimes.

If you don't screw up occasionally, you are not doing enough . . . It's a message we have up on the wall of the offices. "If you are not living life on the edge, you are taking up too much room."

I ran over 25 marathons without a step of training. I never won one, so is that failure? For me it was always a victory just to complete each one.

When I took part in my first marathon I finished. I made it to the end. I survived. I came x-thousandth, but I finished. I didn't win it. I didn't even come 100th, but I finished. So when I did my second one I improved my time. Again was that success or failure? For me it was a great success. I still came way back behind a thousand other people. Everything is relative. And how people react to it.

Paula Radcliffe preferred not to finish at all rather than finish 20th. If she was running in first place and started getting passed by 1, 2, 3, 4 rivals she would rather pull up because she would see finishing 20th as a total failure. Yet if I finished in 20th place I would see that as a miracle, not just a success.

The marathon is a great example of taking the necessary steps towards success. If anyone tells me they can't run a marathon, most of them have never tried. It is not someone who has tried it and failed. But you can get them to break it down. It's just over 26 miles, you can walk 26 miles, you can run 26 miles, you have done it in short batches, maybe not all at once, so what is to stop you putting it all together.

All you have to worry about is the first step, and then the next one at any given point, and the next one, and you will do it.

All these things that seem insurmountable are often not; 99% of achievements are about starting off. People just don't know where to start, so take your objective, and draw it back step by step. Closing a deal doesn't sound bad, all I need to know is where the deal is. Having three deals, my 1 in 3 success rate, that doesn't sound so bad, so how do I get three deals? Well I need to put out 30 offers: that sounds a bit tougher but OK, I need to make 50 phone calls. 50 phone calls sounds a lot but actually a phone call is an easy thing to do 50 times, and then I know I am on my road to getting my success.

You break it down. A step is not a big deal. Running a marathon might be, but a step isn't. So roughly 48,000 more steps and you finish the marathon.

There is always a choice between safety and risk – being prepared to fail opens up a greater range of options

How far does failure and success impact on safety and risk?

As far as risk in business is concerned, all you are doing is gambling, gambling with money to make money.

When you start with an idea, you either have to put money into it, or you put your time into it. If you are putting your time into it, you can't put that time into something else, therefore you are using your earning potential, so you are reducing your income in a different way, by not spending your time on something that could earn you money.

It is an investment, whether that is time or money, and that is a gamble, that is a bet. You can do all the research in the world but at the end of the day it is still a gamble because, if it wasn't a gamble, if it was a no-brainer, then everyone would do it. If there was a guarantee in life that when you put a pound on the table it became two, then everyone would do it. Everything is a relative gamble.

Sometimes you feel that you have some extra knowledge that reduces the gamble. So, for example, if I was placing a bet on the cricket and I knew Jimmy Anderson had a dicky leg and couldn't bowl properly, I would have augmented knowledge that would help me decide where to put my money.

"Those who never take risks can only see other people's failures."

Paulo Coelho

When I start a business it's because either I have knowledge that I feel gives me a disproportionate advantage in betting my money on doing this rather than someone else doing it, or I have a passion that means that the amount of effort and focus I will put into it is disproportionate to what someone else would put in, and therefore I am likely to get a better return. But it is still a gamble.

When I am on Betfair I might read up on the team sheet, I might look to see who won the toss at the beginning of the game, who will bat first, bowl first, what the bowling attack looks like versus the chance of rain, and is someone going to win or is it going to be a draw because of the weather? I will try to amass enough information to mitigate my risk as much as possible, but then to all of that data coming in, I apply gut feeling.

"Gut feeling is a ton of experience. A ton of experience earned from failure."

If you have not failed, your gut feeling is a pretty simple thing. It just says everything I have done in the past is correct, so whatever I will do in the future is correct, which is clearly not going to be the case for very long.

Amass the information, and then always make your decision at the last possible moment where it will still be efficient. In this context, efficiency is defined as the point at which further delay becomes a negative to the outcome as opposed to a positive. In other words, delaying a decision when there is the possibility that further information may change the decision is the objective, but if the decision is, for example, to turn left and run 100 m or turn right and run 100 m and you need to arrive before a certain time, too much delay would mean it's impossible or you are less likely to be able to cover the ground in time. That is the point at which delaying the decision starts to become less efficient.

Mitigate failure by trusting your vision – surround yourself with great people to help navigate the route

You can change the way you view failure by having the vision to know what you will do if something goes wrong. Like the fire in the Paris operation, you can't plan for every single eventuality, but you will know what to do when you have to change tack.

The analogy I like to use is a sailing one. Recently we were out on the Solent racing in a regatta. It was a very windy day and there were four legs to the race. Clearly, if you are doing four legs of a race and coming back to the start, at some point you are going to be sailing against the wind because it is only coming from one direction. We can't define where the wind blows, but we are in total control of the sails.

And Murphy's law says that something *is* going to happen. Murphy's law says that when I want to sail from A to B the wind is going to be in the opposite direction. But if you have put yourself in a boat where you can move the sails around, you might have to tack a few times, but you can sail against the wind. Completely against the wind.

And then if I can make sure I have a couple of really good quality sailors who can help with their experience to sail better against the wind, I am even going to de-risk it further. Getting experienced people, people who have failed before. Which goes back to the point of, "Tell me about your failures." We don't need to know the detail of what we are going to do, we just need to have the confidence in believing in what we are going to do. Once you believe in it, you can then plan all those different things, all those scenarios – and it is completely irrelevant which one you end up doing. The only thing that is important is doing it.

*   *

When I moved with my mother to Zimbabwe at the age of 7, I started playing football for the first time. Within a year I was in a trial match for Rhodesia Juniors, and was switched in at right back.

Five minutes later a long, high ball came over. I had a choice to make. There was the safe one: trap it, or the risky one: try a spectacular volley. I clearly remember watching the ball coming towards me, and while it was in the air thinking about these choices, realizing all I needed to do was not screw it up. I could have let it drop and trapped it, but I took the risky option – and it came off. I scored the goal.

You have got to take the risk and therefore risk failure, because the last thing I want to feel is that I didn't take advantage of the very few years I have on earth. If you feel you have wasted your time, that is a failure that cannot be excused. Now that would be a failure in anybody's book.

The failure factor #forgetstrategy

@GETRESULTSBOOK

The only way to avoid failure is to do nothing, but then again, in that case you will have failed yourself

As Winston Churchill said, success is not final, and failure is not fatal: it's the courage to continue that counts

Roadblocks in life are not there to stop us. They are there to help us measure our conviction to success

Science is essentially a litany of failures, each one leading to the truth

Fail at the hurdles, win at the goals

You can reduce the risk of failure by placing trust in your vision and surrounding yourself with great people to achieve it

"Mistakes are the fees we pay for living a full life."

Sophia Loren

5
FAITH

"I don't use analytics to make decisions, only my gut feeling and intuition. I use the analytics to monitor my decision along the way. Stats can tell you anything you want to know."

The Problem: *Spoilt for choice*

Towards the end of 2006 I was attempting to recruit a head of media. The final choice came down to two candidates recommended by the headhunter I was using: one already had the right experience and credentials, the other was a project manager from Cable & Wireless. For the job itself I went with the candidate who had the media experience. At the time the business was still in recovery mode and we could not afford the luxury of making errors of judgment in our recruiting. However, I had really enjoyed meeting Rob, the guy from Cable & Wireless, liked him, and didn't want to lose the opportunity to work with him. I always recruit on my gut instinct and there was something about him . . .

The Solution: *The leap of faith*

Although I could not offer Rob the media position, I went back to him and said, "Rob, I really like you. You haven't got the head of media job, but I would still like you to come and work for me." "Doing what?" he asked. "I don't know," I said.

Rob was puzzled. "So you're saying you want me to commit to working with you: leaving a well-established company for a small private one, for about the same money, but with at least two hours a day extra commuting – and you can't actually tell me the job I will be doing?" "That's right." "Sorry, Mike, it's too vague, it's not for me."

I was still determined to keep him involved. "I tell you what, come and join us at our Christmas party on Thursday. Meet the rest of the team. I won't tell them why you are there – I'll just introduce you as my friend."

Rob agreed to come along to the Christmas party. It was at Asia de Cuba in London. We had drinks and dinner, laughed a lot, and Rob chatted away with the team. I didn't even get to speak to him the whole evening until it was time to say goodbye around midnight. The next morning he called me up. "I have no idea why I am saying this, but having talked to the guys last night, I am going to say yes."

When Rob joined in the New Year, I started him off looking at our internal networks, but come the end of February, just as we were getting ready to press the button for our IPO the following October, I asked to have a word with him. "Rob, I'd like you to stop what you are doing and run this IPO process for me."

This time he was not just puzzled, he was completely shocked. "Are you crazy? I'm a project manager from a technology company. I'm an engineer who knows nothing about investors, financing or IPOs, and you want me to handle the most important event in Telecity's history in the middle of an economic crisis?" "Yep." Still shaking his head, Rob accepted. That was his leap of faith.

The Outcome: *Onwards and upwards*

I was delighted, because I knew that with Rob's logical, questioning engineering brain and his lack of directly relevant experience – and precisely because of that lack of experience – he would go through every single aspect and detail of the IPO, querying everything, discovering the negatives, solving them, and that he would make it happen. He did a truly amazing job. Citibank and Deutsche Bank both told me that in their experience it was one of the smoothest, slickest IPOs they had ever been involved in. And that was run by a man who had no prior IPO or financial experience.

Rob learnt so much about investors and analysts from that year that I made him temporary head of investor relations while I was looking for someone else to take the job on permanently. He did a great job for the first nine months of the company's post-IPO public life. Even then, the candidate I brought in to do the job on a permanent basis came from a completely different background, having worked at the cigarette manufacturer Gallaher. Rob went on to become the Chief Operating Officer of Telecity, the number three in our company, overseeing an annual department budget of over $200 million. Recently he took over as UK MD, running 45% of the total company. Some leap of faith . . .

* *

I had faith in Rob's ability, based on my instinct that he had what it took to undertake such a critical task for the future of the company. In part it was the very fact that he would not be going through the motions of yet another IPO that told me he could deliver, in the same way that I asked Matthew (who I had brought in to take over the running of investor relations) and James to oversee the acquisition and integration of the data centre company we acquired in Istanbul. In both cases, once each of them had accepted the challenge and understood that I had faith in them, they had a desire to prove to me that my faith was justified, and took the extra steps, and invested the extra energy and commitment to demonstrate that.

Once anyone in that situation gets beyond the initial fear factor, what they are trying to do is prove they can do this task better than anyone else could do it. They want to make an impact. They don't want me to turn round and tell them, "That was great, but the guy before you was better." They will change some element, or way of doing something, or make it personalized to them. And they will strive even harder to do a better job.

"I call this standing on groundless ground – that's when you have got to have faith."

There is a general consensus that everyone has around 33% discretionary effort available at work beyond simply getting into work, doing the statutory 9 to 5, doing what you have to do. If you can give somebody the motivation that takes them beyond that, you are in a position to unlock that additional 33% discretionary effort.

Think of it this way: in a company with 12,000 employees, imagine what that 33% additional effort means: either another 4000 more free employees – or the 12,000 but for the cost of only 9000.

I manage with the belief that there are no bad people, that everyone is perfect for something. It is simply a case of pointing them in the right direction, and you will then find that good people don't need managing at all.

It is a question of judgment. In any situation you have that gut feeling about the probable outcome even before anything happens. That is built up through the experience of asking the right questions and finding the answer, and finally saying, "I don't need to ask the question. I trust my own judgment."

"You must trust and believe in people or life becomes impossible."

Anton Chekhov

Respect everyone, hurt no one, regret nothing

Surround yourself with people who are better than you, give everyone respect, and they will respect themselves *and* you.

In one of the techniques I learned from the yogi Jagdish Parikh, he asks you to state three things that you fundamentally believe in.

My "holy trinity" is "respect everyone, hurt no one, regret nothing." Sometimes these elements conflict, so you have to make a call between them, but that's life.

The faith in other people derives from everything I have talked about earlier in this book. Recreate the mindset. I don't believe in strategy. I have an ethos. I don't write five-year plans. I share and impart the vision and the ethos. You can share that but you cannot *impose* it. Values are personal. You can't tell people what to believe in.

That's why I don't use analytics to make decisions. I trust my gut feelings. Intuition is the only thing I use to decide – analytics and statistics are useful to track what you want to do. Keep your head up. Look at everything else. Above all, trust the flashing warning lights that are the intuitive bad feelings.

That is why I do not need to know what every person on the team is doing every day. And why I happily allow my team to use Facebook during office hours. Not to do so is short-sighted. Why not maximize the value of your team? If a company is prepared to entrust their staff with their function but not to trust them to use Facebook responsibly, what kind of message does that send out to the staff?

From the belief invested in them, they will go on to develop faith in themselves, their own decisions. When I ask someone to take on a task, a job, a project that is going to push them way beyond what they currently consider to be the boundary of their capability, I am at a point of trust in advance of their own trust of their decision. I am already trusting them but they don't trust themselves; not just yet.

When they are ready to take up the baton and sign up to the challenge, a vital element is that it is now time for them to rely on their own gut feeling, not mine.

If they relinquish responsibility to my decisions at every stage of the journey, they will be learning, but they are not exercising their gut feeling muscle.

Because I encourage them to rely on their judgment, what they then start doing, without realizing it, is searching around through all those pockets of their memory for the bits and pieces of track record, empirical evidence and historical data they can find to give them an informed opinion.

Simultaneously, my informed opinion is that that individual is already a good enough person to take a judgment on what any decision should be. They may not think so yet. But I have a different set of data, and I think they are ready, so I tell them, "Go away and make the decisions you need to take." Through doing that, they begin to think, "Maybe I am." It is transference of faith.

After making that decision it is essential not to intervene too quickly and to be prepared to shoulder all the consequences. You have got to let it run. If they come and ask for help then I am instantly there, with no recriminations, because we went into this project together: we went in 100% and we will fix it together.

If they do not call for help, and there is a problem, it is their responsibility to get it back out and do it right. Or not – and then they are free to come to me and say, "I did my best." Nine times out of ten, if I have employed people who are better than me, in the jobs that they are doing, then their best has got to be better than mine anyway. Otherwise I have employed the wrong person.

Imagine I have brought in a team of builders and labourers to do some work on my house. I am not going to go and lay the bricks better than the brickie. If I have honestly hired the best person I could find in the first place and something has gone wrong, well, it would have gone wrong for me too. Probably even more wrong. Why on earth would I be able to do it better?

"In my experience, the greatest successes often have little to with business skills, but having the faith to take a risk."

Faith crops up when you least expect it

The wonderful thing about the opportunity for acting on faith is that you never know when it will surprise you.

A few years ago I was chatting, as you do, to my hairdresser while she cut my hair. I had followed Jackie as a loyal customer through a couple of salon changes because I really liked the way she cut my hair. This particular day I could sense that for some reason she was not at all happy – which was unusual for her; she's normally so upbeat – so I asked her what was up.

She told me that she had always wanted to have her own salon to allow her to get away from the politics of working for some-one else. She had the core desire to make that move but was genuinely afraid to take the leap of faith. I told her that the first thing she needed to do was stop worrying about doing it. Worrying about doing or *not* doing something is a double negative. Either decide not to do it (and live with the relative mediocrity of being less than happy working for someone else) or decide to do it. Then at least the worrying can be valuable.

The next couple of times I had my hair cut Jackie and I talked through the pros and cons of going it alone, and the risks and rewards that she might experience. The third time I went in she told me, "Mike, I've done it! I gave in my notice and this is my final week." Nervous excitement surrounded her like an aura (or maybe an afro!). Having resigned, she already had her eye on a small shop just a few doors away from where she was currently working. We looked at the financial numbers and I told her that she needed to keep faith in herself. She was very good at her job and significantly she had loads of drive and ambition.

The risks were significant for her. She secured the lease on the premises nearby, which led to a battle, as she was going to be taking market share in the form of customers from her previous employer. It was a tough period, and the business showed a negative cashflow for the first year. Jackie had to borrow against her mortgage. But there was also progress. Slowly but surely, week by week, customers starting coming to her. Three years on she had five employees and was doing really well, but most importantly she was happy and fulfilled. I still visit every month.

The key here was crossing the chasm in one leap of faith. Giving up your job, re-mortgaging your house, taking on liabilities and challenging a major competitor – all in one go – is a daunting combination. But it all started with Jackie's decision to do it rather than to worrying about doing it, having faith in her own faith, and taking that first crucial step.

Keeping the faith

Keeping the faith is an integral part of operating in volatile market conditions.

One of the things that Matthew, our investor relations director, spends much of his time doing is helping the market understand our business and ensuring expectations are aligned to our ability to deliver; what we want to aim for is always to try to meet these expectations and ideally slightly exceed them. However, every time we overachieve, the next time the market makes its analysis its attitude is, "Ah yes, they are going to overachieve so we will expect the same again." That makes it ever more difficult for us to continue overachieving. Success drives greater challenges each time.

So Matthew is striving constantly to manage investors' and analysts' expectations relative to our evolving view of the world. Internally, each time the new objectives come out, he starts off by saying that the numbers are challenging and will be difficult to achieve. But gradually he adjusts his belief in our ability to deliver the numbers, and eventually he says, "I think we can do it."

I will go back to Matthew and say, "This is what we are going to do," to which he counters, "What justification or foundation is there behind what you are saying?" ". . . Did John F. Kennedy ever have any justification to say we will be on the moon within ten years? He had no idea. But if you don't put the stake in the ground, for sure you are going to miss."

I don't know how much of it is luck and judgment, how much is good gut feeling, and how much is the sheer determination to deliver. But every time we have achieved it, beyond the initial expectations of Matthew and team. And Matthew has learned, against his naturally cautious instincts (and I am grateful he has those instincts), to share my belief.

Matthew has remarked that he understands that what I try to bring to the relationship with investors and analysts is that sense of belief, that I am someone they can believe in and hence they can believe in the company. That self-belief sets an expectation, gives other people confidence and belief. That is significant because TelecityGroup exists in a crowded world: in the context of all the other companies out there, although we are a market leader in our sector, enthusiasm, energy and self-belief helps to set us apart.

Face to face improves faith to faith

I have already mentioned that I am a great believer in face-to-face meetings, even though a phone call, e-mail or Skype conversation might, on the surface, be more efficient. I also travel a lot, which naturally prompts people to ask me why I do that rather than video-conferencing. We have videoconferencing in every facility, which is invaluable for technical teams comparing notes and completing and cross-checking specifications. But, personally, I find with videoconferencing that I can't read the body language; I can't really look the other person in the eye.

When I visit the countries where we have operations, I fly out and talk to my country managers. I won't even meet them in the office in the afternoon. I will go straight to my hotel, check in, catch up on some e-mails. I will meet the country manager for drinks and dinner, just the two of us. We will sit and talk about all sorts of things all night and the next morning I will fly back.

Whenever I go to Paris, I get a Eurostar to the Gare du Nord, walk across the street to a restaurant we always go to, Terminus Nord, and meet my French country manager Stéphane there. We have the same *plateau de fruits de mer*, and three and a half hours later I walk back across the street, get on my train and return home.

That is the only way I interact with the managers, because it is not about what they write in a report, not about the easy things, it is about the issues they are *not* comfortable with . . . And because they may not be comfortable talking about them I have to tease it out of them. You don't charge straight in and ask a question. You have got to open the oyster to extract the pearl, put people at ease, make them feel comfortable if their guard is up. That is much harder to do down a broadband line.

From their point of view I think that the fact that I, as CEO, have taken the trouble to go to see them, and to spend one-on-one time with them, prompts them to think, "Mike is as rare as gold dust to get time with, but he is as keen to meet me as I am to meet him . . ." When I turn up in Istanbul, Frankfurt or Paris, and ask "How are things, how's business?" they generally open up straight away; they try to throw me as many factoids that they think will hook me within that short period of time. I am prepared to listen to everything. I don't even know what I am listening or looking out for – but I will find out soon enough.

Hire the best talent you can locally in a foreign market, and trust them completely. You can share the vision but you can't insist on how it is implemented.

Trust is based on sharing time together, building that trust. The first time I met the England rugby player Lewis Moody was when we were both invited to an event with Lazards; it was at a private dinner with ten people. We hit it off, and I invited him to an event I was organizing.

I am sure that Lewis's natural feeling was "He wants to invite me along to something as Lewis the Rugby Hero," but the reality was that it was because I liked him and got on well with him. I said, "I want you to bring your wife. This is for you as a couple, we are going to have fun," which we did. I invited him to our wedding, and eventually he clicked that this wasn't about me wanting something (although when I have got a box at Twickenham with guests and he is commentating I'll call him up: "Oi, Lew, get down here I want you to meet some guests," so I have ten rugby balls and he comes down and signs them all).

So when Lewis asked me to get involved in a charity event, the Yukon Arctic Ultra Challenge, a walk across 300 miles of frozen wastelands, raising money for HIV sufferers and children with

HIV from birth – a charity he was clearly passionate about – I said we would sponsor him.

He ended up getting frostbite and had to pull out for that year, and felt he had let everyone down. I told him, "That just shows how difficult it is, and I am sure you will do it again." Lewis is such an amazing and resilient guy I am sure he will do it.

The point is that there is no one-way traffic in a relationship, it has to be two-way, and once you have exhibited the two-way value then the trust starts to build.

In business, there is room to build that trust but, under pressure and in a tough commercial environment, that sense of trust can easily be squeezed out. Goodwill is in short measure. There has recently been a movement to restore "kindness" to business, David Jones, chairman of the Havas advertising group, coined the phrase "Who Cares Wins" to show how that spirit of faith, trust and kindness can actually lead to good business. A recent poll found that the brand attributes which consumers found most important were – yes – "kindness and empathy," and a friendly and socially responsible attitude.

There is even a trend towards following a strategy of "random acts of kindness" when businesses surprise their customers with unexpected, thoughtful gestures. The Dutch airline, KLM, have a team that finds out which of its customers are planning to check in online and then learns out more about their personalities and likes on social media so that they can meet them at the airport gate and give them a small gift: it might be an iPad cover or some golf balls, nothing too expensive but definitely thoughtful. The recipients are always pleasantly surprised to have this personal touch during the frequently impersonal, tedious business of taking a plane flight.

Interestingly it not just the consumer who benefits. The company's staff become more motivated and see their employer in a kinder light. And all those passengers who receive a gift from KLM go away with a little glow, a positive feeling about KLM, and start texting and messaging all friends to tell them about this brilliant airline. Very good PR, and sound commercial sense.

Tell your vision through stories

There is great value in telling stories. And that is the same whether we're talking about management or sales. We sell ourselves 24/7 – that is all we are doing. Even when you are selling a product, the best way to sell a product is to sell yourself. If you can engage someone to the point where they believe you, they have trust, they will assume that having confidence in you means that you are not going to sell them something they don't need. Therefore if you say they should buy this it is because you honestly believe it, and if they believe you – why wouldn't they? And then it is just a question of price.

Constantly selling yourself is the beginning of everything. Telling stories is the best way to do it.

I think we have lost a lot of that in the modern world and the internet has played its part. We have lost some of the ability to impart a story verbally.

A matter of weeks before writing this, I had a meeting with one of my management team. The company had just emerged from three or four months of intense activity, which had built up to a crescendo in order to reach a certain point so I could convince the board to do something very specific.

Part of that had been controlling my mood with my management team: I had been very tough with them, very demanding. It is unusual for me to be like that and, when I am, it permeates like a virus.

It's true even outside work. My wife Shalina tells me that if I am grumpy, my kids get grumpy; if I am happy, they are happy. And everyone around me is the same. If I walk into a room and I am bubbly the room flies. If I walk in and I am miserable – I may not even say a word to anyone – you can feel the room fold. Even I can see it.

So, after successfully resolving this issue earlier in the week in the board meeting, we held a two-day session with all the company's country managers and everything was super-positive. We were flying again.

Despite that upswing, one of my team wanted to see me. She was trying to persuade me to give her an extra staff member, and I wanted her to rethink her strategy.

"Look, you are about to do something that not many people alive today have done: taking a company through an IPO and on to a FTSE100.

"Remember Shakespeare's *Henry V*? There's this brilliant scene where he's just about to fight the battle of Agincourt. He's there with 8000 English against 35,000 French, maybe 50,000 depending on which chronicler you believe. His army has been travelling on foot for three and a half weeks and fought two battles; the men are cold and hungry, and many are dying of dysentery. In front of them are arrayed the chevaliers of the French on fresh horses. The English soldiers are moaning about not having enough people and not a hope in hell. Henry says:

> *"If we are mark'd to die, we are enough*
> *To do our country loss; and if to live,*
> *The fewer men, the greater share of honour."*

The message I wanted to put across was this we are going to do this despite the fact that we don't have everything, because we want to be amongst the few that take the glory for this. And the fewer there are of us, the greater the share of glory.

After she heard that, my team member went out inspired. Now, I could have told her, "I think we are going to be fine next year," but telling the story from *Henry V* brought a lump to her throat. So, who is going to gain the most here? Is it the person hearing a nondescript, "Don't worry, it'll be fine," or someone who has had the vision of Agincourt evoked?

*   *

Towards the end of my time in France, I was about to leave the company I was working for and was involved in a dispute over the payment of the last few months' salaries. I was living in the Loire Valley near Angers. Every day I was doing hundreds of kilometres, commuting back and forth to Paris in an old Jaguar XJS. The car's engine finally blew and I could not afford to get it fixed because I was virtually broke.

There I was, with no money, running up debts, running out of food, not able to pay the mortgage. So I went round the house gathering up all the foreign currency I could find, checking jacket pockets, down the back of the sofa. This was in the days before the Euro and, as usual, I was travelling a lot, so I was able to rustle up a motley collection of Italian lire, German DM, Dutch guilders. I put the lot in a large bag and hitch-hiked the 300 km to Paris.

That same day I had a meeting with the lawyers to discuss the dispute, expecting it to be deferred as usual. To my surprise the final settlement was reached there and then, but even so I would not be able to get the money due for another few weeks. Somehow I had to survive financially until then. After the meeting I went to a nearby Bureau de Change and converted all the other currencies into French francs.

Then I hitch-hiked back to Angers, got a ride in a truck and asked to be dropped off at the last shop before my house, which was an hour's walk further on. I spent those francs on bags and bags of potatoes and other simple foods, and carried the plastic bags home, cutting into my hands all the way. We lived off those potatoes, rationing them out every day, until the money came through.

What kept me going through that difficult time was faith: faith in myself, faith that in the dispute I was in the right. I didn't know that on the particular day I hitch-hiked to Paris everything would be resolved, but faith carried me on, and I took the risk. Afterwards, when everything came good, I felt that rush of emotion, and that sense of the greater glory. It was my own Agincourt moment.

The faith factor #forgetstrategy

@GETRESULTSBOOK

Faith is about taking a step on a ladder where you can't see the rung

---

If we truly knew all the answers in advance, the world would be a very sad place – all scope for courage would vanish

---

Do we ever know someone completely? Almost certainly not: so we need faith in personal and professional relationships or we'd be very lonely

---

The fine line between success and failure is a tightrope we choose to walk in all aspects of life

---

The reason we refer to "leaps of faith" is because deciding to believe in anything without evidence is a jump from the rational to the unknowable

---

A bird leaving the nest has the choice of staying inside or testing out its wings: it has the faith that they will allow it to fly – and fly it does

---

"When is revolution justified? When it succeeds!"

John August Strindberg

6
FORTUNE

"You are at least as likely to have good fortune by doing good things as by doing bad, and you will always sleep better . . ."

The Problem: *A vicious circle*

In 2000 I was sorting out ICL's mainframe maintenance company in Copenhagen. At the time ICL was a UK-based mainframe manufacturer – it made and repaired mainframe computers, that was it; and mainframes were a declining industry. The company wanted to change the business model, and move into outsourcing and managed services. But most of that work in the UK was with government departments and, as often happens, they could not get on the list of approved suppliers in Denmark because they had no track record in offering those services in that country. No track record, so no references, so no clients, circling back to no track record. In their efforts to crack this, the company had already been through four managing directors in three years. All of them had failed, and miserably, to turn the business around. The team was deeply demotivated.

I knew I had to win them over. An important lesson was brought home to me when I was working late one day and I heard the cleaner – who was an employee of the company, not an external sub-contractor – pushing a Hoover and coming closer and closer down the corridor. When he reached my office, I said "I'm sorry, would you mind not doing this right now? Could you possibly carry on a bit further down the way, because I am trying to concentrate?" He looked me straight in the eye and said: "Look, I trust you to do your job, which is to run this company so that I continue to have an income. You trust me that this office is going to be good and clean for your meetings tomorrow so that it creates a good impression for your clients. Let me do my job and I will let you do yours." It was a refreshing attitude. He quite rightly expected as much respect from his boss as I expected from him. I knew I had to spin things around.

The Solution: *A true Christmas tale*

It was coming up to Christmas, a couple of months after I had arrived in Copenhagen. I bought a map of Denmark, on which I plotted the home address of each of the employees who had kids and rented a Father Christmas outfit. All weekend I drove around Denmark, visiting every staff member's house delivering presents, with a big sack of sweets for their kids. I remember one house where there were twins, four or five years old. I turned up early in the morning so they were still in their PJs, and could see me through the semi-opaque glass of the front door. When the door opened I ho-ho-ho-ed. One of the twins jumped up and down in excitement: "Juleman, Juleman! Father Christmas has come." The other one screamed and ran away in fear.

The news spread like wildfire about this nutty new chief executive the company had acquired.

The Friday night before my Santa Claus trek, I had been trying on the costume in the office. I had hired the big furry grey trousers and clogs that he wears in Denmark. One of the sales managers happened to pop by and asked what on earth I was doing. I explained, and he told me his wife worked in a local hospital on the ward for alcoholics. Would I visit them? Of course. That evening I went with him to the ward. It was a moving experience. The patients were crying, holding my hand, grateful that anyone would bother to come and visit them at Christmas time. Some of them, the medical staff told me, were unlikely to make it through Christmas; a dismal prospect.

Afterwards I ordered a taxi to take me home. The taxi driver who picked me up was a little perplexed at my costume. As we chatted about this and that, I told him what I was doing and that really I was a technology company CEO. I also mentioned that I had studied with the Magic Circle. He told me that, in addition to his work as a taxi driver, he was a ventriloquist and a clown, and spent much of his life travelling Africa and Asia with his wife, bringing happiness to impoverished children. He only came back to Denmark every nine months or so to earn enough money to continue his mission.

I gave him my card. A few months later, out of the blue, he phoned me up, "Hi, it's Jon Christensen, the clown taxi driver. They are opening a new children's ward in the state hospital. I'm doing a show: do you want to come along?" I put together a trolley load of laptops, games and other goodies donated by the likes of Microsoft and Fujitsu. Pushing the trolley I made my entrance in a puff of smoke.

The Outcome: *The magic of happenstance*

The next day I went into the office. The opening of the ward and my visit to the hospital had made the national press and the TV news. One article said that the image of a chief executive tends to be heartless. But this shows you can be nice as well. The Danish Department of Health saw the news coverage and got in touch to say they were running a tender for an outsourcing role but had not considered ICL because they didn't think ICL outsourced (which was true). But, as they put it, anyone who cares that much for kids in hospital is going to do a good job.

Even though I did not have a track record or references, and as long as they carried out due diligence, they were willing to give me a try.

The tender was closing the next day – we entered a pitch, and we got the deal . . . The longer-term result was that we now had our first customer and we were able to use the Department of Health as a reference point to start the process of migrating the entire business over to being a managed service provider.

The vicious circle of not being able to get a government client had been broken, by extremely atypical means. The outcome was not planned; it had broken the circle without me trying to, maybe because I was not trying to.

Serendipity was the key, and aiming high.

*　*

Think through the chain of circumstance. If the cleaner had not had the courage and clear-mindedness to remind me about the importance of respect, I would not have decided to go on my Father Christmas tour of Denmark. If I hadn't been changing into my costume in the office, and not had the conversation with that sales manager, whose wife worked in the hospital, I would never have gone to visit the patients in the ward, and subsequently I would never have met the taxi driver, who would never have known I did some magic. Only because of his knowledge of me and the opening of the hospital ward was I able to do my magic show, which happened to be on the TV that evening and the newspapers next day – and only because it was a few days before the closing date of the Department of Health tender did we even get a chance to bid.

Perhaps not surprisingly I believe in happenstance and providence. If someone was to calculate the odds of all of that happening I couldn't imagine the size of the number. Yet this kind of thing happens a lot. It starts with you being open. Being different. Saying yes. Being positive.

Only when you actually commit to something where you can't turn back, fortune helps you achieve what you could never imagine would happen – because by committing yourself to a route, suddenly everything becomes very possible. I first heard this concept expressed clearly during a management seminar, when the presenter quoted a passage often attributed to the German writer Johann Wolfgang von Goethe. Following that moment of definite commitment, the quote goes, providence will start to move, and a stream of events will happen to help you achieve your goal, things that otherwise would never have occurred.

I had decided to make a commitment to turning the Danish business into a success. And it happened.

> "I believe that I am guided by chance encounters. I believe in the miracle of chance encounters."
>
> Paulo Coelho

I often hand out DVDs to my management team, films that contain a powerful message. Recently I gave them all a copy of

The Pursuit of Happyness (and yes it is spelt with a "y!"): the movie based on the true story of Chris Gardner, played in the film by Will Smith. Living in San Francisco Chris invested all his savings into a new portable bone-density scanner which he then started selling to doctors and medical facilities. But his cashflow went haywire, and he found himself in a major financial firestorm. As a result his wife left him, and things spiralled out of control. He had entrusted one of his precious scanners, the thing he was banking on, to someone who went off and sold it. He ends up homeless, with his young son, trying to get things back together again, selling his blood in order to survive. As desperate as you could be.

And then, one day, completely by chance, he sees the scanner being carried by a somewhat deluded man who believes it is a time machine. He manages to retrieve the scanner, repair it, and sell it. It marks a major turning point in Chris's life. At the end of the film we learn that he went on to found his own very successful brokerage firm.

For me the story of the film revealed the ups and downs of fortune, the random chance of Chris bumping into someone in the pell-mell of the City carrying his scanner. It was about the hardships and challenges and sacrifice that somebody has to go through to achieve a goal. Throughout, Chris persisted in believing in himself and his ability to change his scenario. And the more he did, the more fortune he encountered.

Realize how lucky you are

In the current economic climate, everyone in the Western World seems to be feeling miserable, depressed, unlucky, under the cosh.

The very fact that you have bought this book, are reading this book – and *can read* this book, in a country where learning to read is obligatory through mandatory schooling; that you may be sitting on a bus, train or tube, confident enough to be travelling on public transport to work – is placing you in the tiniest percentage of the world's population.

Wake up, review the perspective, and understand what luck really is. It's time to realize how lucky we are:

If you could fit the entire population of the world into a village consisting of 100 people, maintaining the proportions of all the people living on earth, that village would consist of:

- 57 Asians, 21 Europeans, 14 Americans (North, Central and South) and 8 Africans.

- 52 women, 48 men. 30 Caucasians and 70 non-Caucasians.

- 30 Christians, 70 non-Christians. 89 heterosexuals, 11 homosexuals

- 6 people would possess 59% of the wealth and they would all come from the USA. 80 would live in poverty,

70 would be illiterate, 50 would suffer from hunger and malnutrition

- 1 would own a computer. 1 (yes, only one) would have a university degree.

If you woke up this morning in good health, you have more luck than one million people, who won't live through the week. If you have never experienced the horror of war, the solitude of prison, the pain of torture, if you're not close to death from starvation, then you are better off than 500 million people.

If you can go to your place of worship without fear that someone will assault or kill you, then you are luckier than 3 billion (that's right) people.

If you have a full fridge, clothes on your back, a roof over your head, and a place to sleep, you are wealthier than 75% of the world's population.

The word "fortune" leads to "fortunate": my wife Shalina has an Indian family heritage. Spending time in India has made me understand how different lifestyles can be, how fortunate I am. In the same spirit I visited, with my senior management team, the concentration camp complex at Auschwitz. The scale of that horror – made unbearably real by the small, human details: the piles of spectacles, suitcases and shoes – clearly sets any short-term, superficial, self-centred dissatisfaction into the most acutely stark of contexts.

Fortune also suggests "wealth." I recently came across these Six Principles of Life and Money. They were on one of those e-mails that are constantly being forwarded around the business world and wider cyberspace (like the 21st-century equivalent of the chain letter). Who knows where they originate from? But people respond to the thoughts they contain. This one struck a chord with me. So, to the anonymous author of them: thank you for putting these into circulation. I agree with them all.

1   There is no point using limited life to chase unlimited money.

2   No point earning so much money you cannot live to spend it.

3   Money is not yours until you spend it.

4   When you are young, you use your health to chase your wealth; when you are old, you use your wealth to buy back your health. The difference is that it is too late.

5   How happy a man is, is not how much he has but how little he needs.

6   No point working so hard to provide for the people you have no time to spend with.

But if we are lucky, we must not be complacent. There are real issues growing and waiting ahead.

Always be ready to respond to luck and turn it to your advantage

I appreciated the benefits of a lucky break early on. I had finished my apprenticeship in Rockwell Automation and had been moved on to a role as a technical manager – as usual, with no experience of ever selling anything. The company was struggling and sales were proving extremely difficult. Nevertheless I got straight onto the phone.

On the list of prospects was a company based in Wales, who had just got to the end of reselling the old Commodore computer range (remember those beasts?). They liked the concept we were offering and I ended up selling a job lot of 120 computers to them as their first order as a reseller – at a time when the company I was working for was lucky to sell ten a month.

At that very point the managing director of the UK subsidiary of the French company I worked for fell ill. The French did not want to recruit a new MD and my name, at the critical moment, was up in lights. At the age of 21 I found myself MD of the UK subsidiary of a French computer company.

Some years later, when I took over Redbus, it was burning cash at the rate of £3 million a month, with only £6 million in the bank, stripping staff to reduce costs. The situation looked impossible.

Then serendipity intervened. We had just built a brand-new data centre in Prague, opened by the British Ambassador with great fanfare. The site was unlikely to do anything but lose money for several years due to it being ahead of its time in terms of internet take-up. Within weeks the great rains and floods that afflicted Prague in 2002 swamped the building. I went to the insurance company and cut a deal, essentially saying, "Give me £8 million and I'll go away, rather than insist on the £40 million cost of reconstruction." That gave me enough cash to stay alive until the next round of investment came through.

When luck offers you a helping hand, take it. Napoleon considered that one of the attributes a good officer should come armed with was luck. He was reputed to say, "I don't care if he is good. Is he lucky?"

Lay the ground for future opportunities

I almost wanted to add another F to this chapter title and call it *Fortune & Frogs*. Because you need to kiss a lot of frogs before you find a prince, and you never know in advance which frog is going to be the prince.

This is something I have articulated to my investment community when talking about acquisitions. We had just completed two acquisitions in Finland, and a third in Istanbul. The question put to me was, "Are there a lot of other opportunities like that? Let's do more." "Yes," I said, "There are plenty of opportunities, but the difficulty is moving them from being nothing more than an opportunity to a commerciality reality." There are always so many reasons why we wouldn't do a particular deal: the target company might want too much money, or once we are inside and looking at the figures, they are not as good as we had been led to believe. Either way, you have got to kiss a lot of frogs.

We make these acquisitions and we know our competitors are muttering to themselves, "How did they find that one?" It's because we are out and about on the ground. We are alert to these opportunities 24 hours a day. By kissing more frogs we have created a greater good fortune. You do what you can. The more time you put in, the more fortune you achieve.

Every so often we organize a tell-and-pizza session at Telecity. For a couple of hours at lunchtime one day one of the senior team will talk about what they do. An invite goes out: if you want to know more about what investor relations is all about in your business, come and listen. Finance, IT, HR all have their turn.

I did the presentation at one recently: if you want to know what the CEO does, come along. It was full. Everyone wanted to know: what the hell does this guy do? I showed them the details: the 900 hours I spend in a plane each year, how much time I spend in airports, the 831 meetings. The message to them was that you have got to put in a lot of miles.

It is the same with skiing. People say, "I'll never be good at skiing, I am not following the teacher." The only way you can get good at skiing is by skiing. Getting miles under your skis. You can read every book under the sun about how to ride a bicycle. The moment you place your backside on a bicycle seat, you will fall off. That's a fact. You can read the theory as much as you like. It is all about doing it. You have got to get out there and do and do and do.

Chance plays its part, but you will dramatically increase your odds by disseminating and gathering information.

Actively increase the luck your organization acquires, through creative networking, recruitment and training

How much of business is conversation upon tumbling conversation? My wife sometimes asks me why I go to so many networking events. She knows I do a full day's work starting at 7 a.m, get through a raft of meetings, conversations and tasks in the day and then frequently attend five or six events each evening, every week.

I go to those events because I know that the concentric circles that make up my work and non-work life will overlap. At one party I might meet someone who has seen me at a previous event I organized, and who is able to help me with information on a deal that I am trying to do. I didn't plan to meet them. It just happened to be because we were there in the same space, the same continuum.

After the party, I'll spend time catching up with contacts who are passing through London: perhaps a friend from New York – a friend because of doing business together – who is involved in high-level debt funding from New York; if you need anything from the billion dollar mark, there are not many people who can immediately allocate it. He can. I might not need his help right now, but you have to tick these things over, keeping everything alive.

The principle in networking is not that you are expecting a specific outcome. You have no real idea whether the person you are talking to could be useful to you down the line. What you are doing is nurturing a relationship that may come round to help you later on. If I do that ten times maybe three, maybe five, but maybe only one will come around. How can you quantify that? You can't.

You may not know the possibilities and the outcome, but you do understand the context, who will be there, and what they can contribute. You can hit off on a conversation that might be completely at a tangent to the previous conversation, because you have an idea how you can tease information out from that person. It's also about where you can contribute, because if they don't perceive the value of talking to you, they won't engage with you. They are not going to waste their time, so there has got to be a perception at least that you can offer them similar opportunities. That is the game, the dance, the constantly revolving wheel of fortune. For me, it is all about friendship and trust.

Most people will say hard work creates luck: I say don't forget the role of qualities like humility and generosity

I keep coming back to this: surround yourself with good people. To me, "what goes around comes around" means that if you mix in circles of intelligence, inspiration, of kindness, it leads to good fortune.

If you surround yourself with people who are negative, cynical and depressed, what is going to happen to you? You are going to become negative, cynical and depressed.

Therefore, if you surround yourself with people who are benevolent or innovative or inspirational, you are going to become those things. In business I look for the best people I can find because working with them enhances my own capabilities. I look for people who not only have great skills, but who have a kind of aura around them – a sense of gravitas perhaps, but also a little sparkle, a can-do attitude, that "something special". When I mix and network with people I naturally gravitate to these types of people, without knowing who they are or what they do. They are people with a certain aura, which I tap into. It's like a fuel for me.

A couple of years ago, my daughter won an award as the most polite pupil in her school, and that made me intensely proud.

Of course I want her to be successful academically, but that award was the pinnacle. I was telling this to a senior executive at the CBI, who said that this was very interesting because they had carried out an analysis of what skill sets businesses ideally wanted to see in inbound graduates. And the funny thing was it wasn't all about accounting and finance qualification, it was politeness.

* *

I heard a story about a Chinese emperor whose castle was in a walled city. He was quite a compassionate ruler; his advisors were telling him that people within the city were dying of malnutrition and disease. He said he wanted to go out among the people and experience the conditions they were living in for himself. His advisors thought it was probably not a good idea, but he said, "They won't know who I am. I will dress in rags, go out there and live with them for a month." He did this against their better advice and, while he was living with them, he became ill from drinking contaminated water, struggled to eat, and was beaten up for his rags.

At the end of the month he returned to his castle, shocked. "That was the most unbelievable experience. It was terrible, we need to change and fix many things. Now I really understand, I really know how my people feel." And one of his wiser advisers said to him, "You know what? All of the time you were out there you knew that at the end of one month you would be back, whereas for these people there is no way out. Their only way out is death". So even when the Emperor thought he was experiencing his people's reality, he was not, because the observer changes the observed. The very fact that you possess the knowledge that a particular situation is short-term means that you view that short-term situation in a different way.

Every year I spend a night sleeping rough to raise money for Action for Children. It is a strange but rewarding experience: after the preliminaries, at midnight you are out there sleeping down by Tower Bridge, on the ground. It is uncomfortable. It is raining. There is noise all around, police sirens keeping you awake. You have to be careful that people are not going to rob you. In the morning your shoes are soaking wet with dew, even if it hasn't been raining. And it really feels terrible. All next morning I am stiff in the neck. But it is only one night.

So, you have a job. But perhaps you don't like your job: because it is not challenging or because you do not think you are getting paid enough. However, these very dissatisfactions identify in you the ability to aspire to something better.

And the fact that you can aspire to something better says that you know that you can get out of what you are in. Or at least you have the wish to. And having the wish is enough to get out.

Opportunity comes by being open to opportunity. It is around us all the time. Fortune is a pathway to opportunity, and vice versa. It is being open to opportunity that is the difference between taking it or not.

The fortune factor #forgetstrategy

@GETRESULTSBOOK

Once you make an irrevocable commitment to action, you'll be amazed how fortune falls into line behind you in ways you could never have imagined before that commitment

Always remember just how lucky you actually are: even if events seem to be running against, you are fortunate to have the chance to change them

Kindness in business, and qualities like humility, generosity and politeness will lead to good fortune in the future

Opportunity comes by being open to opportunity: it is around us all the time

If you want more fortune, take more chances, turn up more, be more active, do stuff: Fortune likes all of that

Success depends on fortune and chance as much as hard work and knowledge. Anyone who says otherwise is deluding themselves

"You will never find a rainbow if you are always looking down."

Charlie Chaplin

7
FORTITUDE

"If you learn to accept and deal with the pain, it loses its power to hurt you."

The Problem: *It's war*

In 2003 I found myself at the epicentre of one of the ugliest boardroom battles ever to hit London's Square Mile and, as a consequence, learnt what business pain can be all about, and how much fortitude is needed to get through to the other side. There was a tug of war over the internet hosting company I was chief executive of, Redbus Interhouse, a struggle which was ferocious, fanatical, a full-blown war of high-rolling thuggery and skulduggery. The cast of characters – and at times it did feel as though I was playing a part in a fictional mini-series – included Cliff Stanford, founder of Demon Internet (all his phone numbers ended in 666), John Porter, the son of Dame Shirley, plus a Russian oligarch and one of the founding owners of The Cuckoo Club. In particular I had to live with false, embarrassing stories in the press about sexual affairs and mis-management, all of which were completely untrue but which caused huge pain to my family and pressure on me to call it a day.

Alongside this, the reputation of Redbus was at breaking point. The company had become the laughing stock of the industry. Some of our customers were openly ridiculing us, saying that the situation was so bad it couldn't possibly be true. With the staff well aware of the rumours flying around, at the same time as I was being grilled by the HR director about the serious allegations in the press, I felt totally isolated. It was not a good place to be.

The Solution: *Overcoming demons*

My desire to give up and move on was great, but I stayed. I knew the experience would always stay with me and ultimately strengthen both me and the company. Many chief executives would have tried to deal with the threats and the plots behind closed doors or move on to a saner, safer place of employment. The then head of the National High-Tech Crime Unit quizzed me on my personal commitment to seeing through the resulting legal proceedings. I told him that after the hell all of us had been through, we were more determined than ever to succeed.

The Outcome: *Stronger than before*

After one of the messiest boardroom battles of any public company and a string of battles at Extraordinary General Meetings, we eventually ousted the two major shareholders and had one arrested and found guilty of his crimes. We had been vindicated. I engineered a take-private of Redbus, then emerged via the Telecity merger with a group that had a market capitalization of over US$2 billion and more than 90% of the UK's internet traffic flowing through our Docklands facilities.

In 2005 TelecityRedbus was named the Best International Turnaround in the London Business Awards. "Turnaround" was the keyword, though not necessarily in the sense the judges intended it. The episode had marked a turnaround in my own ability to deal with intense pain and stress. Like a freshly-hammered sword plunged into water to harden it, I emerged stronger, ever more determined, fortified.

"Fortitude is the marshal of thought, the armour of the will, and the fort of reason."

Sir Francis Bacon

* *

Getting rid of what is dragging you down

The strength we have is often undermined by past conflicts, old fears, unnecessary worries.

I came across the perfect word for this. I was talking to someone who had just returned from travelling round Asia. We were chatting about all the challenges that he had experienced. He told me he had started off with a suitcase and slowly ended up throwing most of what he was carrying away. It was too heavy, too bulky; he couldn't jump on a train with this suitcase. He ended up backpacking. His suitcase had become an impediment. And then he said someone had told him the word impediment comes from *impedimenta*, Latin for "baggage."

I thought that was superb. When we talk about the baggage that we carry around from our past, we are talking about the impediment that stops us from going forward. Instead of using the product of our past to drive forward, we very often use the product of our past as baggage to prevent us moving forward.

Going forward requires fortitude, and never giving up your belief. In the early days of TelecityGroup I was talking to one of my management team in Holland, sitting in a small Portakabin outside one of the data centres. I told him, "One day this stock will be worth four pounds, mark my words." At the time the stock was less than five pence. "No, Mike," he said, "I don't believe you. You must have been smoking something in one of the coffee shops on the canal."

I asked him, "Why are you accepting defeat on day one? There is nothing we shouldn't be able to do. At least, if we can't do it today, we should be making steps towards it, because the more steps we take towards it, the closer to it, by definition, we are, and if we are closer to it, the possibility of achieving it keeps improving."

At that point there was no hope of us hitting £4, but doing the things every day that led towards improving the company, and making it more valuable, meant that after 6 months, 12 months, 15 months, we were that much closer. We reached £1, then £2, and finally that £4 mark. In 2013, Telecity's stock hit ten pounds.

* *

When Aron Ralston found himself trapped under a boulder for five days on a cliff face in an isolated canyon in Utah in 2007, he had to make a terrible decision: to amputate his own right arm using a fairly blunt pocketknife, or die. He wrote about the experience in the book *Between A Rock And A Hard Place* – a great title – which formed the basis of the award-winning film *127 Hours*.

Having survived – even after taking his arm off, he still had to climb out of a crevice and rappel down a cliff face to get help – Aron Ralston talks about the release of the moment when he used the knife (with which, when he was convinced he would die, he had previously scratched an epitaph into the rock trapping him) to cut through his arm.

His fear was massive but, as he was hacking through his arm, he did not feel the pain at that point because he was focused entirely on the liberation it was going to bring. "With each cut, between the blood and tears, my joy grew, realizing that as my arm diminished my freedom began . . ."

As he cut through the sinews the pain suddenly kicked in, a searing fire shooting up his arm, more extreme than any pain he had ever experienced. It lasted for a second and then a sense of happiness washed over him, because he knew that the sensation of pain meant he was now free. It was his final connection with his oppressive state. "I felt pain," he said, "and I coped with it. I moved on."

With luck, none of us will have to sever our own limbs to avoid certain death. But metaphorically we may have to. The more of these experiences you go through, the more resilient you become. It is like flexing a muscle, your resilience muscle. The more you do it the more you believe you *can* do it. Most of the resilience that we deploy and that we need is only about the belief of doing it.

Learn to turn off the pain and relieve the stress

Pain comes in many, many different forms.

The most excruciating pain I ever felt was having to tell my children that I was leaving home. They had grown up being used to me travelling for a few days at a time. But this time was different. I wasn't coming home again. I had decided to leave their mother. Having my young daughter dragging on my leg as I walked across the lawn to the car destroyed me. I cried. A lot. But, conversely, when my parents died just a week or so apart I felt only a numbness. Emotional pain is complex. Physical pain is easier to deal with.

You can learn to shut off physical pain. Focus on the fact that it is not you. The finger, the limb, not you. Aron Ralston's story is all about this realization.

Run through this sequence in your head, interview yourself. If you wear a watch, is it *your* watch? So, the watch is yours, not *you*. Where is it? It is on *your* wrist? So the wrist is yours, you are not the wrist. And where is your wrist? On your arm. But who is saying that? Your arm is not you. If you have got a pain in your arm, mentally you can detach from that, even though the nerves are telling you not to. Does somebody who has lost a leg become less of a person? You could argue that, in the strength they require to evolve a new life, they become *more* of a person but they still don't have a leg. So their leg is not them. Therefore, you can observe physical pain as a third party.

With emotional pain we have far more difficulty in making that separation. But again the tools are very simple to understand, if more difficult to deploy. If you can detach yourself, think about the "Love it, leave it or change it" proposition.

The Indian Yogi Jagdish Parikh taught me to hypnotize myself to sleep immediately, whenever I need to, to block out physical pain, instantly reduce my heart rate, just by being aware of one's self. He calls it "Managing One's Self."

One of the hypnosis-related techniques I have learned is to touch a particular point when you feel things going a certain way. When they grow anxious in a meeting, some people's legs start twitching: you can see it happening and you know they are experiencing anxiety. The trick is to learn to recognize that, or something similar, as a signal from your own body. A signal to activate a controlled, calming reaction. When you cough, as second nature you put your hand up; it is a natural reaction. So finding your leg twitching – or whatever your personal stress signal is – should immediately trigger an anxiety reduction action.

Here is the thought process. You are in a meeting. Why would this be stressful? Even if you know nothing compared to the people around you, even if it is about not hitting your target, you are there to do a job for which you are getting paid. And if the job was that easy you would get paid less, or someone else could be doing it.

You are there because you are valuable. You are getting paid to fix this problem. So why would you be feeling anxious about it? You should be feeling privileged, excited about the fact that you have a role in life. Whatever problem you are facing, it is simply an obstacle, and as Sébastien Foucan, the creator of freerunning says, "In freerunning, as in life, it is always the obstacles that determine who you are."

Identifying the trigger and immediately reacting against it leads to de-stressing, and removing fear. If you are getting stressed out, trying to race to a meeting and the traffic lights are all against you, the hypnosis technique allows you to trigger a state of calm.

Another element of dealing with pain in business is doing everything in your power to alleviate the pain. If we take the scenario of you dreading a meeting coming up because you are not hitting your numbers, fast forward to the consequences. What are the consequences of not hitting your numbers? Well, you are now a year ahead and your share price is going to go down because your investors are not going to believe in you. They will say you are not managing the company well, or perhaps that the market has conspired against you, that you could have done this or done that.

Which sounds the better of all those scenarios? The market has conspired against me, that sounds bearable.

But wouldn't it be better for you to say I have done everything possible in my control and the market is still negative?

How do you do everything in your control? How do you satisfy that outcome? What is really in your control over this? Your sales are down. Have you actually done something about your sales team? Have you done everything possible to improve the marketing? Have you changed your product? Because if you haven't, then do it. And if you have, you know what the outcome is going to be. So don't waste time worrying about it.

You might want to consider pre-empting the pain by leaving the company. The point is, once you start putting things in a trajectory, everyone knows what the outcomes are going to be of any situation that they fear. There may be five outcomes, two outcomes, or just one, but you can envisage most of them.

Behave with grace under pressure

I talked earlier in the book about the phrases "Hard work creates luck" and also "What goes around comes around." I don't believe in the concept of "What goes around comes around" as some external force, but it definitely does ring true when you realize how many opportunities you gain through connecting. You have to be seen to be taking the opportunity. I could go to all the events I attend and never utter a word, and those connections that in due course may lead to business opportunities would never arise.

It is important to attend networking events, conferences, industry seminars – yes – but being engaging, contributing, listening and having an opinion is what provides the differential. It is not bad to have an opinion, even if other people disagree with it. Or just saying "Really?" and asking a simple question to probe, to open up a debate. Extracting someone else's opinion is just as valuable, because they are connecting with you.

However little you feel of your opinion it is *your* opinion, because of the way you have grown up and the experiences you have had, or not had. If you are in a meeting thinking that this person opposite you knows everything about one subject, still speak up. If you perceive your opinion to be stupid in their presence, so what? You have had a different upbringing. You have not spent 20 years studying that one thing. For you to come and volunteer an opinion is perfectly natural.

There is nothing you can say that is not right and proper as long as you are being respectful and polite. By voicing your opinion you should be enhancing your knowledge because there is going to be a response, and you will feel better for saying it. If you don't say it you are likely not to be better than you were before.

The corollary of this is that in business you should surround yourself with better people than you. I necessarily view things from my angle, while you might not look at it that way. I may be sure that my way is right but I only have one angle on life. With the experience I have I might be in a better position to have an informed opinion, but that doesn't mean that your opinion is less valuable, and certainly you as a person are no less valuable.

And through your lack of experience you could still come out with something through your innocence that is valuable to the situation. At the very least you need to take the time to listen to other people.

Very often we talk about issues at such a micro level that we forget the broader picture and the fact that other people do not share the same depth of knowledge. Every time the company comes up to a full year or half year result, I know I am going to have to go on the BBC and CNN. Beforehand, I book in a session with a former journalist. I will have spent the past six months speaking to analysts who insist on knowing every single detail – because they are building complicated models – but at the half year and full year 99% of the people watching the TV interview don't even know what a data centre is, and may not even care: I have to make that interesting too. Every time we come up to an announcement, the journalist and I have a session and he brings me up to scratch on the big picture again.

I start off every time with, "And we have added 27 mega . . ." and he interrupts "Stopppp . . . Bring it up, because the people you are talking to are at a different knowledge and interest level."

I firmly believe that however difficult a business situation you are in, however highly charged, you should retain politeness and grace and reasonableness – even more so in complex, fierce fights like the Redbus situation I was caught up in. When I had to resolve a staff poaching issue with the head of another company – and we were already at the legal letter stage – he and I were able to have a measured, non-confrontational conversation because we had happened to sit next to each other at a dinner a few nights earlier, and had been polite to each other and, through that, we had made a human connection.

Don't be afraid to stand up for yourself. Life is not about getting knocked down, it is about getting back up again when you do get knocked down. But I often say to myself, "How bad can it be?" Remember the importance of understanding our basic good fortune; where so many people who are already in the top micron of a per cent of the population of the planet always focus on the negative.

Part of this attitude is understanding that other people have different levels of fortitude and stamina. I am lucky. I have a lot of stamina and energy, and I do everything in my life with maximum effort. But I try never to judge other people by my own capabilities because I know my own capabilities have changed over time. I do not expect my team to do what they do in the way that I do. If they can't function without sleep then we won't get a good result.

Building the strength to adapt

I recently attended a governmental discussion group on education. There were senior people there from universities describing their view of the future. When it came to my turn, I said, "First of all nobody has mentioned apprenticeships. You are saying that all the universities are churning out graduates and yet there are no jobs. What is that telling you?"

The average ten-year-old today, by the time he or she retires, will have had 40 jobs, compared to 25 years ago when that ten-year-old would expect to have no more than four jobs in their whole career. So if you are already pigeonholing yourself with a degree in one subject – and some degrees, from my point of view as a businessman, are extremely spurious – what does the future hold? Not a great deal. The strength to adapt, to change course, is vital.

There are thousands, maybe hundreds of thousands of bankers out there with no jobs now. They are having to retrain for the first time in their lives, having to come to terms with the fact that they need to do something other than the one thing they thought they would always do. They are struggling.

Add to that the six million English-speaking graduates coming out of China every year, let alone India: the latest figures predict that, by 2025, India will be the most populous nation, not China. All of these people will be coming out with English-speaking degrees, each year more than we have in the entire UK university system. Where is the value-add of just having a qualification? The future will be about moulding a solution, creating a portfolio of knowledge assets, having the flexibility and vision to put that knowledge to work.

"So why wouldn't you just teach people how to adapt themselves, how to learn, how to evolve?" I asked. I was an apprentice. It was a great experience. Part of an apprenticeship is that you go round each of the departments of a company: you learn some accounting, spend time with the sales team, gain experience in panel beating, production or QA and, before long, you are an incredibly valuable member of that business because you know how all these elements fit together. And, in addition, even if you went into the company with one intention you could come out of it with another thought process because you found that your particular skill set was actually more appropriate to a part of the business you had never thought about.

Then, later in your career, if you do have to change path, you have experience of all those different roles, and they don't scare you. "Oh, I haven't been in finance before." So what? You have. There is no magic formula. It's hard graft.

"Life is not a problem to be solved, but a reality to be experienced."

Soren Kierkegaard

The fortitude of tough choices

These stories are reminders that we still have to fight to win, that we must never get complacent.

I had to learn about fortitude early on. At the age of seven I moved with my mother to Zimbabwe – still Rhodesia at the time – to escape my father. He had drifted to the wrong side of the law, as well as being violent towards my mother. When he went to Australia, my mum took advantage and we legged it to Rhodesia. This was the era of Ian Smith, UDI, economic sanctions. Life there was difficult. At various times we were petrol-bombed and shot at, in convoys travelling between cities.

When my father returned to the UK and realized we had disappeared, he expended a huge amount of effort to track us down. He bribed emigration officers to try and discover out which country we had gone to, came across a photograph of me in the garden of the flats we lived in, in the Rhodesian capital Salisbury, and hired a helicopter to look for the buildings. When he found them, he came over, and tried to strangle my mother. We managed to get him deported but, before long, he had forged a passport and re-entered the country with a disguise. These were strange, stark experiences for me as a kid – for any child my age.

I learnt a lesson about tough decisions while I was in Africa. I remember being at a friend's bungalow, in their large open-plan kitchen, with double doors opening to the garden. I had grown very used to the harmless lizards who would pad across the floor while we were watching TV, so when I saw a tail poking out from behind the pedal bin I was not bothered. My friend's mother asked me to get the lizard out because she wanted to close the double doors. As I moved to the bin, it turned out this was no lizard: a spitting cobra reared up, as tall as me, and stared right at me. I knew the cobra was deadly, could shoot two jets of venom into my eyes in an instant. I was transfixed, petrified, frozen in shock. Out of the corner of my eye, I saw my friend's mum pick up a broom, smash the cobra and throw it against the wall. "You could have done that," she tutted scornfully, and got on with preparing some food. I could have done it. I should have done it. She was right.

I applied the lesson from then on. When I took up an apprenticeship, working from 6 in the morning until 9 at night every weekday, and going in on weekends for the overtime, I would rollerskate ten kilometres down the A5 in Milton Keynes along a dual carriageway because I couldn't afford the bus fare.

After I joined Redbus, one of first tasks I had to address was to cut the staff from 400 to 80 – an 80% cut in the staff level: horrendous. It was late in the year. I had the option to release them before Christmas or keep them on one more month. I preferred to make them redundant before Christmas and give them the one month's extra money – it was the best I could do in the circumstances. The reaction was often virulent: "I hate you – you've ruined my Christmas." The decision about who to keep was a tough, tough one. I could have cried every day for a week.

But I knew I had to concentrate on the 80 who were staying with the company. I kept on one woman, but had to let go of her husband and brother. What I learnt was that those people, the ones who had lost their jobs, discovered their inner fortitude. That woman's husband is now running his own business. One of his former colleagues went on to set up a bike company, which he would never had to do otherwise – sometimes removing the impediment, however painful at the time, can release a stronger forward movement.

If you confront the challenge and the pain and find the strength to move forwards, how do you feel coming out of it? The fact that you've got through it is the best feeling in the world. And that makes you feel that you can conquer anything.

The fortitude factor #forgetstrategy

@GETRESULTSBOOK

Resilience, determination and will are far more powerful than physical strength

It is not the falling down that makes the difference, but the getting up again

Fortitude is like a magnifying glass of virtues: your values are magnified through the power of consistency, determination and resilience

Respect the fact that other people have different thresholds of fortitude and stamina to you – work together as individuals not automatons

If progress is painfully slow, dispose of the impediments, the baggage that is dragging you down and diminishing your fortitude

Even when your reserves of fortitude are low, always act with grace, hope and inspiration under the most extreme pressure

---

"If you are going through hell, keep going."

Winston Churchill

8
FOCUS

"I do start-ups and turnarounds. I use a broad brush. I am not a detail guy. I do high-energy, short-burst activity that makes a quantum difference."

The Problem: *Pushing for more push*

Normally, business plans are skewed to achieving a year-end budget. If you look at a graph of sales there's a hockey-stick effect at the end of every year. Then everyone relaxes because they've made the target and four months in they're already behind budget and starting to panic again. I think much of this attitude arises from our inherent habit of burying our head in the sand when it comes to being faced with a challenge or daunting task such as beginning the year with a stretching target. We hope that by ignoring it it will disappear . . . Well, it usually doesn't. The kind of business at Telecity is of a highly recurring nature: every deal made in January generates twelve months' income; any sales made in December are only one month's income in that year. I wanted to find a way of showing my team how to focus on targets right from the beginning, to engage, and to never be afraid of commitment from the very start.

The Solution: *The Lillehammer Run*

We went bobsleighing at Lillehammer in Norway. I thought it would be great fun. It was more frightening than swimming with the sharks. After three or four initial runs in a slow-running practice sled, we swapped to a real Olympic bobsleigh steered by a professional driver. The twists and turns came up with unbelievable speed. The G forces were well over 4G, equivalent to those that fighter pilots experience in combat. There was one corner on the run where we had been advised to hold our breath or we might black out.

On each run we were given a time split for the push-off to the point where we all jumped into the bob. You could see how a faster time at the start paid massive dividends overall. A 0.2 second improvement at the start translated into over 2 seconds at the finish: a return-on-effort ratio of 10:1.

Another outcome the team articulated when we re-convened later in the day was the inevitability of the situation once they were flying down the track. There was nothing they could do to stop the bobsleigh or positively affect its trajectory: like jumping out of a plane, there was no turning back. But – and it was a positive "but" – they knew it would last less than 100 seconds, so they focused on the finish line.

The Outcome: *Real momentum*

The experience demonstrated that focused effort was infinitely more valuable than effort randomly applied. It also showed that regardless of our fears or concerns about being able to deliver on a specific goal, it is always better to address the issue up front and not delay any course of action available to us. After the bobsleigh runs we were able to keep up the motivation from day one.

The Lillehammer Run was something I did for a very specific purpose, designed for the kind of recurring revenue base that Telecity works round. Not everyone will have that same business model, but there is a broader business application.

If you can see something that will improve your position, your performance (or your life), then do it now. If you are able to push hard at the beginning, you should. If you have pushed as hard as you can push and you are still not making it, and you realize if there is nothing in your capacity to make a difference, do not worry. But if in your heart of hearts you feel that you could have pushed a bit harder then, without agonizing about it, push again.

If you have to sell 10,000 widgets every year, why wouldn't you push most at the beginning of the year? You will probably end up behind target at some point, so if you have done better at the start, that will compensate for the leaner months. And guess what? You might even double your target.

*   *

There are many kinds of focus in business.

I first became a managing director at the age of 22, so I made plenty of mistakes in my early days: frequently they were a direct result of lacking focus. I learnt that lesson fast.

However, especially if you are employing young people fresh out of school or college, their ability to focus is completely different. They have their own kind of focus: so how can you manage these people, these self-confessed scatterbrains?

Release the freedom of the hypertext mind

I talked earlier in the book about how to manage people with hypertext scatterbrains and the need to create knowledge space around values, to articulate those values and your vision, and then rely on them to manage themselves.

The mental functions that are losing the "survival of the busiest" brain cell battle are those that support calm, linear thought. The hypertext mind: my brain is always on, always thinking.

The exponential growth in the impact of technology will continue to change the way we live and work. There are 14.3 billion searches on Google in the US every month. In 2006, the number of searches was 2.7 billion. The curve is still rising.

Studies of office workers who use computers reveal that they constantly stop what they are doing to read e-mails: for every small interruption of thought the cognitive cost can be high. Frequent interruptions scatter our thoughts.

This addresses that element of blurring the distinctions between work and home to gain better value, allowing individuals to organize their own private/work time whether they are "at work" or "at home." As we have seen, there is – increasingly – no distinction between the two, previously discrete, ideas. No one minds working overnight if the next day they are not obliged to come in to the office, if they can work from home.

In order to free my mind, I ground it in time. Every week I am in different time zones, often seven hours one way, followed by seven the other. So I always keep my phone on UK time. I do not set the option to pick up the local time. Everything is a relative point.

I am also – and this is not about technology, but the workings of my bodily system – very particular about when I eat and how much I eat. I travel on planes so often that sometimes I get asked at passport control where I have come from and I genuinely don't remember. I have to look at my boarding pass to check. Food is served on every flight and it is difficult not to take it. On a series of flights in the early morning, I could in theory have breakfast in the hotel, the lounge, and each flight, and be five breakfasts to the good by the time I land back in London. To avoid that, I have to use a different kind of focus, self-discipline. If I am on a plane and know that I am attending a dinner that evening, I will consciously nip to the loo when I see the trolley trundling down the aisle.

Relish fragmentation

Is fragmentation a bonus in business or do we need do find a third way: that somehow increased productivity is a balance between the fragmenting of our time and the logic of the linear process?

I come to this from the point of view of someone whose life is permanently fragmented – something I relish. I fill up my days with as many things as possible. I don't have a PA, so my one luxury is that on a day when I don't have to travel on a plane but am jumping between meetings around London and in and out of the main offices in Canary Wharf, I sometimes have a driver. The time I spend in the car is my e-mail time and my catch-up time, my phone time. But I don't waste any time at all. There is not a minute I waste.

Even when I am travelling by plane I already have my list of things that I can do, that I don't need to be connected to the web to carry out: I will have downloaded agendas, printed out reports, ripped articles out of magazines, I am not going to be online: these are things I can do during that one-hour flight. Prepping to use every minute is second nature to me.

Allow your mind to be "always on"

Some business books suggest that you should switch your mind off from being always on. As you may have guessed from the previous chapters, I would argue that this should be the other way around.

I am always "on" and I enjoy it. I like having the optionality. One way for me to eradicate fear of success within my business is to empower people and then to know that my phone is by my side and it is not ringing.

If I switch the phone off, my thoughts will start drifting to who might be trying to call me and for what reason, but if it is on always and no one calls me, again it is back to the reverse logic of the high jumper. I want to know that no one is calling me . . . And that is what gives me the confidence to sit there not thinking about it.

If I switch the phone off it means I won't be concentrating on what I have in front of me, because I am wondering about what could be happening out there.

Everybody says these things. Most business manuals are about focus, focus, focus. Ignore distractions. Close the door.

When I am in my office, my door is open. Only if I am having a confidential conversation will I then close the door. Otherwise, even if I am having a meeting, the door is open. People come along and, if they have an urgent issue, they can pop their heads round the door, "Mike. I am really sorry to interrupt" and they know where the limit is.

Equally, they know that when the door is closed it is for a confidential issue. So I am allowing them to enter and take part in my world of priorities – rather than them being uncertain where my priorities are. If the door is closed, then it really is exceptional and it is because of the confidential nature of the meeting, not because of the importance of the meeting. This meeting is probably important but you may have something to tell me that is *more* important, and I am empowering you to decide that. The reason that the door is closed is because I don't want them to hear the conversation, not because I don't want to be disturbed.

Skim more, focus less

A 2008 study found that in most countries people spend on average only 19–27 seconds looking at a web page before moving on; skimming is our dominant mode of reading.

Again, the received wisdom is: dodge distractions; read more, skim less. I think completely the reverse. Skim more, read less.

"Engage with everything, and then filter."

As an investor you have to plant many seeds, not knowing which one will flourish. When you get to a certain point, when a few of those young shoots have come up everywhere then you need to filter. Ask which one has got the greenest leaves – *then* focus.

Engage in everything, have a mental filter, and – this is the fear of failure again – don't worry about getting it wrong, because very often getting it wrong is probably not that wrong. Not doing something is very wrong.

And then you can focus. But even when you are focusing if you have done all the other things we have spoken about, how much time do you have to focus? You have pockets of time.

The focus comes in a non-linear way, as I noticed with John Porter, who I worked for at Redbus, and who was constantly on the move: boom, boom, boom. He didn't take one opportunity and go in a linear fashion from here to here, because if the one thing he was banking on didn't sprout, he was dead in the water. Microfocus.

The linear mind would say, when you are planting the seeds, try this one first. If it dies I will plant another one. If you plant 20, one at a time, and each one of those fails for the first 5, you are a disaster. But if you plant 20 at the outset and 15 flourish, and you only need 10 – happy days. Same outcome, different timescales.

No one can genuinely multitask

No one can multitask: all they can do is focus 100% on many things at different times. You cannot focus on two things simultaneously, but you can jump between them faster, which gives the impression of multitasking.

During the course of each year I attend a number of charity board meetings. I will have my laptop on the table in front of me and, as the meeting progresses, I am doing other stuff. I am absorbing the information from the meeting, I am hearing it, and I will chip in when something sparks my interest; but most of it I don't find relevant or interesting. I am sure it is relevant to many people, but I have to find the point where I can add value. With a dozen or more people sitting round a board table, they can't all add value to every phrase or statement; otherwise everyone would be talking all at the same time.

So I listen to what is being said, but only a percentage of my brain is actively doing that. I effectively switch off – or more accurately I disengage – and then I am engaged in whatever I am doing until there is a trigger, like a buzz word, or someone actually focuses something on me. I then revert back and they get 100% of me for a short period, before I drop back.

The same applies when I am back at home. I get changed into my scruffs or into my onesie. The first thing I do almost habitually is set up my laptop and then I will be sitting there, answering an e-mail and leaving it, watching TV, reacting to another e-mail.

I am very productive. I maximize every day. I work in cabs, planes, trains, when I am on holiday (even on honeymoon).

I only sleep two or three hours a night, but I can catnap in the car as well – just drop off for three or four minutes and I am fine. Whenever I go to the theatre or a concert, almost every time I am out for five minutes.

I am always looking forward. But there is a downside. I think there is a part of me that doesn't appreciate fully some of the things that I do. I don't enjoy the moment enough. Again it was something my yogi told me years ago, talking about MBA courses.

If you go to Harvard, they will know you have five hours to do your homework, so they will load you up with ten hours of homework, push you all the time. It is all about getting from A to B faster. And when you've got to B they tell you you've got to get to C, and so on. So when you get to Z, you look back, and you say, "When was I actually happy?" You are not. Because the very moment you achieve, you haven't achieved, you have got another objective: that's good for drive, but your life will be gone without you actually even appreciating it. There is a balance to be struck.

As it happens, the multi-platform, fragmented world we are entering is one that I feel very comfortable being part of, and completely in tune with. Was I always like this? If I try to forget my recent past and go back to childhood, I don't think I was. As I remember I was quite the opposite: very linear, very quiet, very lazy. I would do nothing as much as possible. I only scraped through every exam by 51% by doing a bare minimum of revision.

Then I started working – I'd work from 6 in the morning until 9 at night through my apprenticeship, training people who were earning 20 times more than me. And that was when and why I flipped from being lazy to not being lazy: work. Work changed everything. But even there I still wasn't multitasking. I only had a limited number of things that were in my life, and I wonder now how much certain elements in the next stages of my life – a disruptive family home, divorce – were self-inflicted, to generate turmoil, or to create brokenness. Maybe I don't flourish in static times.

I don't call myself lazy now. Although I criticize myself for not doing things. Whenever I have a spare five or ten minutes here or there, and I catch myself vegetating, I feel guilty, really guilty. After going back and forth to the US three times in two weeks I had a weekend, unusually, with nothing planned. I found myself watching the Champions League final between Bayern Munich and Dortmund on the Saturday evening and I was feeling irritable. Why? I didn't even have a vested interest in one German team or another winning the title.

So I created a vested interest – I went on BetFair while I was watching it, and placed a bet on Bayern to create some tension. I couldn't just sit there and enjoy the match. Value creation or risk. And I remember thinking at the time, "I should be sitting here chilling out, the football is on." But I got my phone out and put a bet on to give me a bit of adrenalin.

These are clearly experiences and attitudes that are personal to me. If you look at your way of operating, working and living, I hope that you will be able to use mine as a reference point, to compare and contrast, and maybe adjust what and how you use your time and your mind that will suit your lifestyle and your personality.

Get your focus right in Q1, don't wait for Q4

Why should there be seasons, and can we disengage from tradition? Is it the baggage – the *impedimenta* – of what we have always done that stops us doing it differently. That is the essence of George Bernard Shaw's phrase: "progress depends upon the unreasonable man." It is about not being impedimented – if that is a word – by the past way of doing things.

When one of my staff is in the middle of working on the day's task and suddenly remembers it's their mum's birthday, I am happy for them to click onto notonthehighstreet.com or biscuiteers.com. They can stop what they are doing, prevent the gift preying on their mind, order it and move on.

It is the same principle as waking up in the middle of a night with a brilliant idea, using a smartphone to capture it, sending yourself a text and going back to sleep, confident and happy that you have freed up your mind by releasing it to the technology.

We can become hidebound, blinkered and stuck in a silo mentality far too easily.

To counteract this, I thought that the company, including myself, needed to be aware of, more in tune with, our senses. This arose a couple of years ago, when two of our country operations were going through the same situation. They had both built an identical software application to serve their local needs, where one of them could have developed the application and the other could have used it for free, and if they were even smarter they could have distributed it across the group.

So I said, "We should make more use of these meetings when we are all together. I know you are all focused on your own businesses, but when we are together be aware of what's going on with everyone else, because although you may think it is not important to you what is going on in another company or country, it could be valuable for all of us."

I took my management team to the restaurant Dans Le Noir. You arrive at the restaurant and, after being shown a menu in a lounge area, you are led into the restaurant, which is pitch black. You cannot see your hand, cannot see anything. In fact you have to leave your watches and your phones outside, because if you have your phone in your pocket and it lights up, you can see it through the material of your trousers. It is that dark. The waiters are completely blind; they are able to serve and walk around the tables because they know the walkways, and they also have headsets. There is someone watching through night vision CCTV, saying "Table 15, turn left, turn right." They serve you the food, bring you a bottle of wine, place your hand on the bottle of wine and say "Good luck."

You have to find your wine glass, put your finger in the wine glass and pour until you feel your finger gets wet, so that's enough, and then you find someone else's. Over time, you grow very used to this. You still can't see a thing, but it's funny, you are all sitting around the table, and if someone speaks to you, you look at them, your head moves towards them. You feel yourself doing this, but you can't see anything. It's a very strange feeling.

You start to attune. You start to focus. Your taste, your hearing, your smell improves, you use your hands much more, because you can't use your eyes. So it's making sure you maximize every sensory value by taking one away. It encouraged the team to interact more attentively with each other rather than focusing on themselves. They had to ask each other, "Who last felt the salt pot? Does anyone have the wine?"

Focus on the positive

I had the chance to be at a dinner where Deepak Chopra spoke to us. The first thing he said was that 99.9% of human DNA – whether you are black, white, Chinese, short, tall, fat, skinny – is identical, and yet we spend all of our lives focusing on this 0.1% of difference, which is irrelevant in the great scheme of things. We ignore all the good stuff – because we bag it: that's good – and then we focus on the bad. But progress of ourselves should be also about exploiting the good, and focusing on the good.

Changing the bad is important, but you don't change the bad by focusing on how bad the bad is. You change the bad by starting with the man in the mirror. And in the end the good will overcome. That is a slightly different way of approaching problems.

Recently I met Floella Benjamin, the former children's TV presenter. She was talking about a positive approach to kids. She had been in a school canteen not long before where three yobs were opening the crisp packets and not paying for them so everyone there was giving them an extremely wide berth. Floella walked right up to them, and in a loud, clear voice, said, "Gentlemen, gentlemen, what on earth are you doing?" She was not angry – the tone of her voice was not "you bloody yobs" – just resolute. "I want *you* to be prime minister, I want *you* to be a doctor, I want *you* to be a successful businessman. And you three are giving people the wrong impression of yourselves by doing this. This is *not* you, but you are giving people a bad impression."

They instantly turned from teenage yobs into five-year-olds and, embarrassed, they left. She had shocked them by not giving out the typical reaction. She had said, "First of all it is probably not your fault, but secondly it *is* your fault from now on and what you are doing is detracting from you rather than complementing you."

If something is going bad, you focus on the negative. The more you focus on something the more you feed it. If you focus on the negative you are going to create more negativity. Surrounding yourself with inspirational people creates more inspiration, focusing on inspiration creates more inspiration.

*   *

At that dinner with Deepak Chopra he had another example. He said, "Take the butterfly. Have you ever thought about what happens in the transformation of a caterpillar to a butterfly?" "Well I suppose they go into a cocoon and they come out." "Yes, yes, but what physically happens, what happens in there? They both have exoskeletons, what happens? Are the wings there in the caterpillar, are they there but not developed? No they don't, the wings don't exist. This is not an evolution of a specific being. This is a complete change. If you think about one aspect – this is the most stark example of this – a caterpillar moves incredibly slowly, while a butterfly flutters rapidly. Think about the heart. It can't be the same. The beating system of the butterfly has to be infinitely faster than the beating system of the caterpillar. So it is physically a different heart, a complete transformation.

"And the way it is generated is that the caterpillar also has what are called imaginal cells. These cells are completely different from caterpillar cells, carrying different information, vibrating to a different frequency – the frequency of the butterfly. At first, the caterpillar's immune system perceives these new cells as enemies, and attacks them, much as new ideas in politics, business, science and medicine are disregarded and often fought against by whatever the current mainstream is.

But the imaginal cells are resilient and the more they are attacked the more they produce, in ever greater numbers. Because of their unique frequency they start recognizing each other and bonding together. As this happens they create bigger and bigger groupings and then the groupings start to merge until the caterpillar's immune system is overwhelmed. The caterpillar's decaying body then becomes a feeding carcass for the butterfly."

There are many analogies about caterpillars being ugly and butterflies being beautiful, but the key point is that if you focus on the positive, it is a lot more powerful than focusing on trying to address a negative. By focusing on the positive, by default you subliminally address, and defeat, the negative.

It's only by the caterpillar's focus on the imaginal cells – which are not even negative, just different – that it destroys itself. And, even more interesting, when the butterfly cells realize that they are one entity, a family, a team, it no longer falls to the tiny imaginal cells to do all the work, as each cell now knows its role in the transformation. There is something to do for everyone. Each cell is drawn to its natural role and all the other cells encourage that. Real teamwork!

* *

When we IPO'd TelecityGroup it was one of the most dangerous times to go public. In the technology sector both SmartStream and Sophos pulled their highly anticipated IPOs within a week of ours. We were the last technology stock to get away in October 2007, and the only one for the following four years.

The message was "Batten down all the hatches on IPOs." There was nothing going to market. Everyone was too scared. But we decided we were going to push on: there was a tiny window, we were going to go for it.

We amassed a cast of thousands. An office dedicated to the process, a long table in the middle, with dozens of people around the table, the big hitters, the best of the best: Deutsche Bank, Citibank, Freshfields the lawyers, Brunswick for investor relations, rafts of analysts, our management team. Assembling this high-powered personnel had a significant cost implication: tens of thousands of pounds a minute, ticking away relentlessly.

The start-up meeting was planned for a Monday morning. I was already committed to attending a friend's wedding in Florence that weekend, and there was a problem finding a commercial flight back at the right time. There were so many people coming to the start-up meeting that I couldn't change the timing, but I was not about to let down my friend and miss the wedding. Deutsche said it was not an issue, and rented me a private jet to get back on time. I would be able to land in London, go and get changed and be there to chair the meeting.

The best-laid plans . . . On the Monday morning there was fog in Florence and we left two hours late, so when we landed at City Airport I had to go straight to the offices and into the kick-off meeting. It was exactly the same as happened when I was trying to get back for the awards ceremony.

Most of these people in the room had never met me before. In I walk – again in my ripped jeans and T-shirt – "Alright, mate?" A senior partner at Freshfields, one of the biggest legal firms in the world (he is a good friend now) took one look at me and said, "Oh, I'll have a coffee, please!" I nonchalantly said, "OK" and went over and got him a coffee. Somebody from one of the other advising firms noticed this and caught my attention. "I'll have one of those as well . . ." I ended up serving everyone coffee.

And then I sat down in the middle of the table . . . Only then did they realize who I was, and that this was my meeting. The reversal of focus was 180° and, as a result, the dynamic of that meeting was electric.

The focus factor #forgetstrategy

@GETRESULTSBOOK

Whether nothing is happening in our lives, or too much is happening, we need to stay focused on the objective

Success is a journey, not a destination: life is full of mini-milestones, allowing us to resolve seemingly insurmountable problems step by step

Unlike the received wisdom that we should always avoid distractions and concentrate more, aim to skim more, read less, relish fragmentation

When you are investing time, energy or money in future projects, plant many seeds and only then focus on those with the greenest shoots

Focus on yourself – if you want to change anything, the place to start is right there!

Focus on being yourself because that is the one thing you are guaranteed to be better at than anyone else

---

"Concentrate all your thoughts upon the work at hand.
The sun's rays do not burn until brought to a focus."

Alexander Graham Bell

9
FUN

"I completely agree with Napoleon Bonaparte:
in victory we deserve champagne; in defeat we need it."

The Problem: *Eyes firmly glazed*

When I was working for Tricord Systems in Paris in the early 1990s, my primary task was to open up the market for super-servers, way back when Windows NT first came out: it was the first multi-processor operating system that could take advantage of a computer incorporating several processors. These super-servers looked like giant toploading washing machines, extraordinary objects. Although I was based in France, I was setting up distributorships around Europe, and put one in place with Unisys in the Czech Republic.

I established the initial contact, went out to Prague, and sold them a number of machines that they were to resell. They asked Tricord to train the sales team. I went back out to run the training and discovered that the sales team was extremely unsophisticated. It was not their fault. The most complex technology that they had been selling previously was fax machines. Now they were suddenly moving onto super-servers, which at the time were the state of the art, and required a high level of technical understanding. On top of that I was talking to them in English, and they were struggling to follow both the language and the high technical level. By the second day I could see them wilting before my eyes.

I returned to Paris with the sense that I had not achieved what I wanted to: which was to bring them up to a certain level where they could talk in an informed, believable way about all the technical aspects of a super-server. If they couldn't do that they were not going to sell any machines, so my distribution was not going to be productive, or profitable.

The Solution: *Pulling rabbits from a hat*

I was working with a Frenchman who was a member of the Magic Circle. I was telling him about the problem I was having with the Czech sales team, and saying that I just wished I could do something to capture their imagination and retain their concentration.

"Why don't I introduce you to the Magic Circle?," he suggested. "I perform at children's birthday parties and the magic certainly grabs *their* imagination. If you are saying that the team out in Prague has a fairly low level of technical knowledge, maybe you should treat them like kids."

Through his connections I was introduced to members of the Magic Circle, where I learnt the four basic tricks of magic:

making things disappear and reappear; card tricks; sleight-of-hand illusion; distraction techniques. Everything you do is a variation of one of those four things. They are relatively easy to pick up on a baseline: the key is making up the story you weave around the core techniques to create different tricks. I worked hard to master a number of tricks and, six months later, found myself back in the Czech Republic running a refresher course. In the interim, of course, as I had feared, they had not been very successful in selling super-servers. They had not taken in much of the information the first time round.

For this session, instead of droning on at them, every time I saw a slight lowering of the attention level, I performed a magic trick. They were wide-eyed, genuinely wide-eyed, and astonished. The presentation was amazingly successful. At the end of the session, one of the salesmen came over to me and said, in all seriousness, "When did you first realize you had these powers, Mike?" I suppose it was a less cynical time.

The Outcome: *Abracadabra!*

Having gone there with the sole intention of keeping a group of people who barely spoke English awake during a presentation on data server technology, by pulling a few rabbits out of hats and making some objects disappear, the session really perked them up, got them listening, and created an immediate bond. In the subsequent months their sales performance began to climb.

I started doing more and more magic – and still do. I will perform it in client meetings, at corporate presentations and conferences. A couple of years ago, I was giving the keynote speech for a conference at the Mandarin Oriental in London. The topic for my talk was how to avoid complacency in business. I walked on the stage and told the audience, "Here are your profits" – at which point I pulled out a silk handkerchief – "and this is what can happen to them if you are not careful" – and made it disappear in front of their eyes.

*   *

There is a totally serious point to using fun as a business technique. Business can be high-level, high-risk, involving millions of pounds, but there is still a proper place for fun, not only as light relief, but because it fulfils a specific purpose and achieves useful results.

Adding entertainment value

I am often asked to speak at an event first thing in the morning. To be a good keynote speaker you need to capture your audience from the outset. That opening speech in the morning must be immediately captivating, because you will find people turning up five minutes after the official start, registering late, grabbing coffees at the back of the room, with doors opening and closing, making disruptive noises that can distract everyone else. By putting them at ease it sets the tone for the whole day.

If I can do that, and maybe drop in an outrageous comment or three in the course of the speech, everyone laughs and settles down, so that the speaker who comes on next is receiving their full attention and good questions straight away. It is a bit like being the warm-up man for a comedy show.

My magic and patter plays a significant role in achieving that. There are other key moments during a day-long seminar where the most important role is to rejuvenate the audience: straight after lunch, and once again towards the end of the day. Perhaps because I offer entertainment value I seem to be taking on those slots more and more.

I was giving a presentation recently, where I brought along a pair of gloves which contain a Bluetooth telephone. You can be walking down the street and talking into your little finger and thumb, because the glove has a small microphone and speaker – you look like part of a Secret Service detail. I was talking to the audience about the new levels of technology, asked them if they had ever heard of a talking glove, and put the glove on. I was not making a huge point, merely that the internet is growing beyond people's imagination. But that moment of fun, of humour, had the desired effect.

I enjoy doing the magic, but from the reaction I get from my audiences, I know they are also desperate for a moment of fun. Attendees turn up to these seminars, sometimes because they have to, sometimes because it is part of their job to be there. Many are genuinely interested, but often they have to go through five presentations before they find one that is relevant to them. Introducing an element of fun into their world should be a minimum that you do when you ask someone to spend some of their time, and it really is *spending* time – you can't get it back. A conference or seminar is a day of your life gone: at the very least you should be finding ways to give value for money. And my personal opinion about giving value for money is if they are not engaged, they are not going to get the most out of it. One way to get them engaged is to make them have fun. It is a driver of that.

Forging relationships can be more important than anything else in business. When you are selling, whatever you are selling – a product, a service, an investment, or yourself – you have to grab customers' attention and then keep them interested: for me one way is to use magic, but it doesn't matter what you use.

"Don't just be noticed, be remembered. It's like casting a spell."
Giorgio Armani

Creating an ice-breaker

As well as the magic, I use a range of business cards to set the agenda. I have, of course, standard business cards, but I also have one that is a pop-up rack of data storage units, and another which is a cartoonist's impression of my head and shoulders. It is designed so you can sit it on a desk. If you scan it onto your Smartphone using an app like Blippar my face becomes animated and gives you a short video presentation about TelecityGroup. Believe me: *everyone* remembers that business card. They keep it in full view on their desk, and the message grows.

Remember that I am running a public company, talking with investors and City analysts. I am not a groovy events organizer.

So when I do go into slightly more conservative environments and if I do feel that that would be too zany, I carry a few others with me. They are pretty avant garde as well. Even the more conventional cards have only my first name on one side, and my surname on the other.

Interestingly this is now the new standard for the company. When I brought that out I was the only member of the team with it, and everyone either said, "Wow" or "I don't want one of those, those are too silly." Now it is the norm. I didn't ask for it to be standard: slowly the company grew into it and one by one, as people renewed their stock, the style changed. Although there was initially some resistance, all of the team as well as clients began asking where they could source similar cards.

Remember how one investor once said that the business model I had evolved at Telecity meant that it "could be run by a cheese sandwich?" Once I realized that he meant it as a compliment I decided I would create some business cards that had a picture of a cheese sandwich on them. As soon as someone asks me why, it gives me an opportunity to tell that story – hopefully raising a chuckle in the process – and to make a serious and important business point about the continuity of the company along the way. It opens a dialogue, and dialogue is the lifeblood of business. I use these fun approaches not just because they are funny but because they work.

It doesn't have to be a business card, but if you can find something along the same lines it means that when you meet new clients or potential business contacts, being slightly out of the ordinary will achieve two goals. It helps to reduce the inevitable initial meniscus of surface tension; and it sticks in the mind of the person you meet long after that first encounter.

Make sure you have fun at work

"Life and work are so intertwined these days. We are always online, always working, 24/7. If you are doing something and not having fun doing it, you are wasting your life."

I am not looking for sympathy when I say that being a CEO is a very lonely role. It is the nature of the job. The buck stops there. Everyone comes to you for inspiration. Everyone also comes to you to moan. And no one does that for me. I have a chairman who is there at a distance, available when I call. He is basically the sounding board for my emotions and frustrations. It's really important to have a chairman that you can rant to from time to time, but is slightly removed from the day-to-day running of the business. The board is not the right forum to air emotional frustrations, so my chairman, along with my wife, bears the brunt of my moods! Equally, having fun at work helps to release tension.

The higher level message is always: I want to be able to say to anyone in the company all the way through the team, "When you come into the office in the morning, whether you are the CEO or you have just started as an apprentice, I want you to arrive at work with the expectation that you are going to enjoy your day and, alongside that, the thought in your mind: 'What am I going to do today that is going to make the company more valuable at 5 p.m. than it was at 9 a.m.?'"

This is what I learnt in Denmark when the cleaner came down the corridor and told me he trusted me to do my job and let him do his. It taught me a lot about the destruction of hierarchy in a business. As a result the management structures of all of my companies are very flat, which makes it far easier to imbue the company with a sense of vision and enjoyment.

"If you're not having fun, you are doing something wrong."
Groucho Marx

Fun feeds into fortune

There is a significant side effect of fun: that it feeds into fortune. I recently had the chance at a charity auction to bid for afternoon tea with Rod Stewart – I know, very rock 'n' roll. We had a delightful tea; I brought along my wife, Shalina, who is a professional photographer; and Rod arrived with his wife Penny

Lancaster, who is also a photographer. Shalina and Penny started talking and making connections.

You don't know how these circles spin off, but the very last thing on my mind when I was bidding at the charity event was that Penny Lancaster would be there to introduce Shalina into a photographic angle. They are loosely connected, but meaningful things evolve.

We happened to be going to see Rod in concert a few months later, and he said, "Why don't you come backstage with your guests?" This gave me the opportunity to give my guests the opportunity of a lifetime by introducing them to Rod Stewart. In terms of corporate hospitality, this was a great coup and very difficult to quantify in terms of value. How the company benefited out of that and whether it justified the original donation that created the opportunity may never be known, but at the very least we should look to have fun whilst creating relationships with customers, prospects, employees and suppliers.

That's also why I like having fun, because it is the best way of building a two-way relationship. It is very rare – if someone asks if we can offer tickets for a particular event in our box at the O2 Arena ("Absolutely, have two") – that I don't hear from them for two years and then the next time it's just, "Can I have tickets for that . . ."

I am happy to be generous, but I also sense I have a cut-off point when I don't feel that someone is being appreciative, even though there is no other agenda than having a good time and getting to know people more.

What is getting to know people? I am friends with many, many people who I do business with. I have thought about this a lot in the past, and I don't think I can actually do business with people that I am not friends with.

Something might happen. It flows into these concentric circles again. All of those things are not happening because there is an objective behind them. They are happening because a) they are fun and b) sooner or later all of these things overlap. Let's say that there are seven billion people in the world – when you reduce it to the people who work and live, for instance, in the Square Mile of London it is less than half a million. When you take out the individuals who can decide on spending x or doing y, it starts to become a very small group.

If you build enough relationships, either directly or through others, the concentric circles of relationships mean you can get to almost anyone. The Six Degrees of Separation principle really exists. It doesn't have to be in the Square Mile, it can be in sport, literature, in any field of activity. When you meet friends of friends within one circle, you frequently find they are also friends of people you know within other circles, and so the ripples continue to spread out.

If I didn't honestly believe it, truly to my heart, that these people were friends and I liked spending time with them, I could consider myself very cynical: what am I doing here, just build-ing up profiles? But it is more than a purely strategic focus. I try not to spend any time with people I do not like.

Unfreeze team tensions

Company bonding sessions tend to receive something of a bad press: exercises run by overly cheerful facilitators involving assault courses or role playing. Is it a junket for the staff, or is there a quantifiable and positive outcome?

I think that, used in the right way and in order to deal with a real, specific problem, bonding and shared fun can help to create cohesion as well as neutralizing conflict. Unleashing team motivation will unlock that extra discretionary effort which is often otherwise wasted. Trust evolves from sharing time together as well as sharing the same vision.

When I talk to the management team about this they say that they recognize the value of the events and trips I organize. The team sessions act as crucial indicators of how the whole company is performing, because we look ahead to the future and agree what we want to achieve. But equally the team appre-ciate that one element is about the company giving something back to them in gratitude for their enormous levels of commit-ment and hard work. Telecity operates in an industry sector where staff turnover is notoriously high. The fact that most of the management team have been with the company for ten years or more says something about the two-way exchange of trust and respect, cemented by the fun occasions.

After I had merged Redbus and Telecity, bitter rivals in the marketplace for many years, I needed the new team to bond quickly and the rivalry to be set aside. In the office, there was a façade of professionalism. There was no overt arguing in meetings, but I could sense the tension, and afterwards some-times overheard a certain amount of bickering and bitching about each other.

I was aware that I needed to snap them out of this potentially damaging attitude, and that to do it I would have to get them out of the business environment. I arranged to take the team off to the Ice Hotel in Lapland.

If you've never been there, everything in the hotel is carved out of ice. The chairs are blocks of ice, the tables, the glasses, the plates and even the beds are made of ice. It's an extraordinary place. There are candles, but no electricity, and since the rooms are clearly freezing cold, you have to sleep two to a room on an ice bed, under furs, using the heat of each other's body to keep warm. Otherwise you will freeze. There is no choice if you want to make it through to morning.

Best of all, for the purposes of what I wanted to achieve, there were no toilets in the hotel rooms – because that is the one thing that would melt. You have to head down a corridor and go outside, in temperatures of −30 to −40°C, in the pitch black.

They say you can't go out without alerting someone in case you trip over and bang your head, since you'd be dead in the morning. You always have to inform another person you are leaving the hotel at night, and so your roommate has to wait and guide you back in. This requires concentrated team work. Whoever you are with, rather than going and finding someone else, they have to be standing at the door: "This way, this way." The person doing the guiding has a vested interest in helping the other one make it back successfully, because it is going to get him or her warm quicker. On their own he wouldn't even have been able to go out.

This gave me the opportunity to place pairs of the more prickly rivals together to share the same glacial bedroom, where they would be obliged to overcome any embarrassment, set aside their historical differences for the more pressing demands of survival.

I added another twist. The team arrived in the morning and I contacted them to say that I had missed my flight and that they should start the meeting without me: I asked them to prepare a summary of what they discussed and the conclusions they had arrived at. One of the team, who at that point did not know me that well, remembers that he thought this was highly unprofessional of me. Only later did he realize it was a ploy. Without me there the team, together in this situation for the first time since the merger, had to draw up their own agenda. The Telecity staff were not going to let the Redbus people set the agenda, and vice versa. They immediately set to work and started formulating, together, a vision of where we were heading.

When I arrived later in the day, and before I told the team what was happening, we went to the vodka bar and had a good few drinks. I needed their guard to be down. I also needed their bladders to be full . . . At the end of the session in the bar I told them what the rooming arrangements were. A few of the team laughed nervously. Nobody said anything out loud, but they were visibly uncomfortable.

In the morning, we all got up slowly, partly the after-effects of the vodka, but it had not been a night of restful sleep: the cold, the physical discomfort of the hard bed, and being woken up by your roommate in the dead of the night to guide them to the loo and back.

We reconvened at breakfast with the ice chairs, ice tables, ice plates and glasses. Everyone had a soft, smiley face. They understood why I had done this. They had overcome their fear of embarrassment and their personal hostility. As Douglas Englebart, the late, great computer and internet pioneer, once observed, "The rate at which a person can mature is directly proportional to the embarrassment he can tolerate."

The team had realized that the individuals that they had previously mistrusted and disliked were in fact "normal" people, just like themselves, who came into work every morning with the same issues and life challenges as themselves, and with the intention always to make the company better, never to make it worse. The needs to keep warm, go to sleep, have a pee, were common to everyone regardless of their opinions, style or company allegiance.

After a couple of hours' work we took some skidoos out on a nearby frozen lake. In the middle of nowhere we parked up next to a little straw and wood hut. Inside two large salmon had been smoked, and we sat around having salmon and schnapps. Everyone was exhausted, but happy. There was no positioning, no tension. Despite the sub-zero temperatures, any awkwardness had melted away. A magical moment.

Back in the office the team felt enlarged, enhanced. If there was ever a resurgence of the old issues, it was sorted out by the team themselves. The speed of interaction was dramatically improved. The team was able to communicate directly with each other. They weren't coming to me individually with all their problems: they now trusted each other to be supportive, and even when old tensions occasionally and inevitably bubbled up they were far easier to resolve.

The fun factor #forgetstrategy

@GETRESULTSBOOK

Life and work are so intertwined, if you are not having fun you are abusing your privilege of being alive

Just because the mechanics, the finances and the systems of business are inherently serious, that doesn't mean you cannot have fun

There is no point, and certainly no pleasure, in doing business with people you cannot enjoy spending time with

By thawing relations between competitive colleagues through shared fun, tension can melt away

Make a positive effort to turn your body's warning signs of distress under pressure into a state of *de*-stress – learn to reset your rationality

We measure our quality of life by its happiness so contributing to a colleague's happiness adds value to the company via their improved performance

"Life is a helluva lot more fun if you say yes rather than no."
Richard Branson

10
FUTURE

"*The ground around us is shifting. For some the future is a frightening place. I disagree. I see and relish a future of immense possibility.*"

The Problem: *Life itself*

I have an absolute fear of being dead. Not of death, the moment, but of not existing. I have always been terrified of that and spent a lot of time thinking about it. I would wake at night, sweating, shaking, with palpitations, emerging from a semi-sleep, semi-dream thinking and worrying about it. It was the sense of the world carrying on without me in it, without me participating in and experiencing it. This lasted for many years. The only way to deal with it was to accept the inevitability of death and the futility of fighting it. You can't control your death – unless you choose suicide or euthanasia, and that is only the method of death, not its existence – but you can control your life.

The Solution: *Using the now to control the future*

Because I do not want to miss out on life, I try to use my days and nights 24/7. If I am not doing something, I feel I am wasting my time. I have a fear of wasting time. I cram it in, I push to stay awake as far as I can. Every now and then I crash for 24 hours. My body tells me to stop and recover. It used to be every nine months or so, then six, now as I get older it is every four months. It is my body's defence mechanism.

Every year I have four board meetings in Hong Kong, where I fly in overnight, arrive at 7 a.m., start the meeting at 9.30 and finish at 6 p.m. before flying back that evening to London. That's 24 hours in the plane for 8 hours on the ground. That's the way I like it. I travel a lot. For the first week every month I watch all the movies on the planes. I don't sleep during flights. For the next week I catch up on all my reading material. For the remainder I work through the whole flight. I have no PA or secretary. I don't believe in the need for them. I can do things faster than asking someone else to do them, and possibly more reliably . . .

The Outcome: *The future is bright*

After all that unquantifiable information, the facts do speak for themselves. Telecity is currently in the top 150 of the list of the largest PLCs in the UK, from being worth around £6m when I took over to over $US 2 billion. It has been one of the most successful companies in the entire stock exchange since our IPO in 2007, and the most successful IPO in the main market since 2005.

Be attuned to what lies ahead

The future is happening right now. There is no point peering into years that lie ahead because by the time you have chewed over and analyzed the potential it will already be the past.

Have a look at these facts – what do they tell you?

- The top ten in-demand jobs of 2013 did not exist in 2004. We are currently preparing students for jobs that do not exist, to use technologies that have not yet been invented, to solve problems we don't know exist . . .

- We live in a time and a world of exponential growth. The first commercial text message was sent in December 1992. Today the number of text messages sent and received every day exceeds the total population of the planet.

- Very shortly a supercomputer will be built that exceeds the computational capabilities of the human brain. It is predicted that by 2049, a £1000 computer will exceed the computational capabilities of the *entire* human species. Think about what Albert Einstein once wrote: "I fear the day that technology will surpass our human interaction. The world will have a generation of idiots."

- It took 38 years for radio to reach a market of 50 million, and TV 13 years to reach the same level. The internet reached that size of market in 4 years, the iPod in 3 years and Facebook in only 2 years.

- If Facebook were a country (as of 2013) it would be the third largest on the planet, just behind China and India.

- Mobile traffic is expected to increase 13-fold between 2012 and 2017, and mobile video traffic 16-fold in the same period, by which time there will be 1.4 mobile connections for every person on the planet.

- In 2013, compared to ten years earlier, the number of searches on Google increased from 55 billion to 1.2 trillion. In 2012 the number of bytes of data created every day was 2.5 quintillion – yes, that's quintillion (or 10^{18}) . . .

- Every two days we create as much information as we did from the dawn of civilization to 2003 AD (caveat: that does not necessarily mean that is better quality information!)

- NTT Japan has successfully tested a fibre optic cable that pushes 14 trillion bits per second down a single strand of fibre. That rate is tripling every six months and is expected to do so for the next 20 years.

Think about advances in bio- and nanotechnology. Then consider the music industry and how slow it was to react to radical changes in the way it operated: the megalithic record companies believing that they knew best and being caught out – first by underestimating, and then fighting, sites like Napster in a battle they could not win – and by the ability of the internet to deliver a music number 1 to somebody posting a video from their garage in Seattle, Seoul or Sunderland. Changes in the way we make films are undermining the existence of Hollywood – an industry that not long ago seemed to be indestructible.

The message to me is clear. Do not dwell on the past. Plan for knowledge change. Embrace, don't fight technology.

"Success lies on the leading edge, not the bleeding edge."

The future is a fragmented but not a frightening place

We have to reprogram our way of viewing the world. Recently I had the chance to talk with Dr Susan Blackmore, who is an expert in memes. She told me that everything around us competes for our attention, even inanimate objects. So these are subliminal messages that the inanimate objects give us, which we are bombarded with on a regular basis and through which we have to navigate in life.

I found this intriguing. It is something that came up when I gave a talk to teachers and graduates in Oxford about the difficulty of educating kids today versus before: what seems to be the case is that historically we have relied on the linear brain pattern; in other words, you learn something that evolves you to something else that evolves you to something else . . .

Today, because of the way kids are brought up, where they could have the TV on, playing a computer game, sending e-mails and texts popping up, all of their attention is fragmented. They are absorbing multiple hours of content every hour. We can't multitask, there is no such thing as multitasking. You can skip between tasks rapidly, but you can't multitask.

Part of the poor performance in education – yes, despite record grades I feel that education fails miserably – comes from not understanding the way the future will operate.

Kids are slicing up their attention. That can be great in some respects, but if you are trying to teach a kid something, how do you teach them? It has got to be completely different to how it was before. Do we actually teach kids the same way, by giving them five inputs at once for them to capture, maybe put them on a roll so they only capture bits at a time. Or do we say we compete only for certain parts of that slice? Take that time slice, then bombard that. The one thing that is important to acknowledge is that it doesn't work the same way as it did before, or it will not work the same as it has done before.

Given the number of jobs a 10-year-old will have in his or her life how important is it that they have to learn in a very structured way? Isn't it more important that they are able to be fragmented and multi-disciplined?

But how are we teaching them? Still in the same linear fashion. We should be fragmenting it and joining it up at the end – and using technology to do that. Starting with the end result and building the way to it, rather than saying here is something and maybe we can make a business out of this going forward. It is about taking everything, every position you have and moving forward.

Is there a limit? Do we want a limit? How do we know when we have got there? When you are always pushing the envelope, how do you know when the envelope tears? You only know when you know. Just like a high jumper . . .

When I was being taught physics at school, a teacher once told me that the only thing you can prove is that something is not true. You can't prove something is true. It is only true to a certain point. If you have a ball and you bounce it, you can expect that if you let it go at one particular angle with a certain speed it is going to bounce up in the same place, time and time again. The theory of probability is that at some point, it could be in 60 billion years, that ball is going to bounce in an unexpected way, because everything happens eventually. So all you can prove by doing this a million times is every time you have done it you have done it. Only at the moment where the ball goes off in a different direction can you prove that the law is not absolute.

By always pushing the edge you never know where the edge is. Until you have actually reached it and then it is often late.

Know what it is you don't know – or "New" is the new "Normal"

This raises another issue: know what it is you don't know.

I always refer to the four stages of: 1 unconscious incompetence; 2 conscious incompetence, 3 conscious competence; and 4 unconscious competence.

The best way to think about it is driving a car:

1 Unconscious incompetence

A child of seven generally doesn't care about driving, they have no interest in how to drive a car. They simply know that if they need to be somewhere, the car will be driven to take them there. They are unconsciously incompetent. They don't know what it means not to be able to drive a car.

2 Conscious incompetence

But then when they get up to their mid-teens, they start to feel it is becoming debilitating not to be able to have a car, because they have friends who can drive, and who therefore possess freedom, mobility.

At that stage they have become consciously incompetent. Nothing has changed but now it has become a problem for them. Not knowing about your incompetence is fine, you are deliriously happy. Knowing about your incompetence suddenly causes you a problem.

3 Conscious competence

Then you start taking driving lessons. Everything seems difficult: there are actions and thought patterns that you have not had to use before. Then you become consciously competent, so you are driving but you are thinking about every aspect: hands on the wheel 10 to 2; mirror, signal, manoeuvre. You have to work hard but you're improving, so you become consciously competent.

4 Unconscious competence.

Then of course, ten years later, you are driving back from work and when you get home you can't even remember the journey – your mind has been so pre-occupied with everything other than driving. You are now unconsciously competent.

That is the dangerous point. Because when you become unconsciously competent almost always the cycle starts again. You become unconsciously incompetent at something that is linked. It is constantly discovering things that you are very comfortable with and finding where the slight tweak on that is that jumps you out of your comfort zone, because you are always unconsciously incompetent at something. In this example it could be that you are so engrossed in thoughts about everything but driving, assuming your subconscious is looking after that, that you don't pay enough attention on the road and have an accident.

It is the step before knowing what it is that you don't know; the dangerous point is not knowing what it is you don't know.

"If you want to make God laugh, tell him about your plans!"
Woody Allen

There is a way of describing the fine line between unconsciously competent and unconsciously incompetent. A friend of mine was looking at a picture of Clint Eastwood as a cowboy wearing a poncho, and he had one piece of straw coming out of the corner his mouth. My friend said, "He looks so cool with that one bit of straw. But if he had two bits of straw – one coming out of each corner – he would actually look really stupid." It was the thickness of a straw that would make all the difference between looking super cool and super stupid . . . A very fine line.

That tiny flip is the difference between the unconsciously incompetent and consciously incompetent. Although the consciously incompetent point is a very scary place to be, it is a whole lot better than what came just before it.

And that is a world that people need to stay away from: the unconsciously incompetent. The best way to stay away from it is by immediately identifying when you are unconsciously competent at anything, and to know that within a very short space of time you may already have crossed the line back to unconscious incompetence.

The future is the possibility of change

The essence of the learning process is of continually moving and adapting to be ready for whatever the future brings, just as much as the course we take.

The upside of this is that people learn to change, are not frightened by change and deal with tasks they didn't even know they could deal with. Most of that derives from the shared ethos, the shared experiences, the shared vision. Because we are that close, because we have been broken down, because we have shared the same experiences. Everyone has the same interpretation of pain, risk, success, challenge, teamwork. A real culture.

I try not to worry, but I am human, and I do end up worrying. It's a process. I try continually to go back and ask, "What am I worrying about? Have I done everything possible to mitigate it?"

At INSEAD I was taught by Jonathan Story, who talked about "The Frontiers of Fortune", the essence of which is about how events that you are not necessarily aware of affect other things. If there is a tsunami, how does it change the price of pineapples in San Francisco? If you follow it through there is a raft of repercussions. Anything you do has a broader knock-on effect than can possibly be conceived. Which again gives us a greater responsibility to do the right thing in all cases. We have a much greater impact than we can possibly know.

We can go through life doing something wrong, thinking "That was my decision, no one is going to get impacted but me," but they always are. And when you do a good thing, that impacts everyone positively around you as well – far more than you can possible imagine.

Relish the immense possibilities the future offers

"How wonderful it is that nobody need wait a single moment before beginning to change the world."

Anne Frank

Planting seeds for the future is almost like being an angel investor. You are an angel investor of time. What you are doing is dropping seed money, seed time money, into many different things and waiting for things to come up. And just like a seed investor, some of them will come up immediately, some will die, some will come up slowly and then suddenly become big. Some will require more of your money you will need to spend some more there to take it to the next phase. That is why people say the biggest funds get the biggest returns, because you have got to put so many seeds in the ground.

On the seeds I haven't already planted I don't actually even know what the future potential is. So I will talk to someone about something, and I am not planning to plant anything, but by having that conversation, I have planted a seed.

I do not know what the flower is going to look like when it comes up. But I know why it is important to do it. I may not know what will come out of the ground, but I know it is important to continue to invest, to continue planting seeds of whatever they may be, because they come round so frequently.

In life, people talk about the unexpected. My wife is from an Indian family. I have found that many Indians do not like planning far into the future. They can't understand that my diary has items in it for two years' time. "How do you know what you are going to be doing?" "Well, the point is I do know what I am going to be doing if I put it in the diary. I build my own future. I shape it." But they say I can't possibly plan that far ahead. Organizing big family events is a real challenge!

You don't need to put everything in the diary. You don't need to plan out your entire life, but as soon as you start to drop things in, you can shape the way it is going. And you know that there are certain scenarios, that you are going to be in this country around that time. You are going to be on holiday at that time. So you shape other things to fit into that. And what you have done is create your own destiny to an extent.

Whereas if you leave your destiny to chance you could be in those places, you could be all over the place. But you know ultimately there are five or six things you are going to be doing in a year's time. You are not going to be an astronaut, so don't plan for being an astronaut. Tick that one off. You are probably going to be doing something similar to what you are doing today.

You might be in a different relationship though. There are your scenarios, your optionality. Which one looks the best, which one would you like to happen? Pick it. Great. Now you know these are the risks, nothing is going to come along and bash you on the back of your head unexpectedly because you have just outlined what the potential scenarios are. Now let's focus on this one. How do you make that happen as opposed to those? What are the steps to get there?

But if the journey goes off tangent towards there, it's no surprise. You knew it could go that way, so bring it back in. You are setting out those roadmaps of life. What you are doing, as well as planning and setting the future, is removing the pain, because a lot of pain comes from fear, emotional pain, business pain: that fear of what is going to happen if I don't hit my targets?

This is ever more important because it is not just that life changes, so of course you have to embrace the future, but that the *rate of change* is accelerating. If it took 1000 years to get a horse-drawn plough, 100 years to build a tractor, 10 years to create DNA-driven plant growth, then it is one year to the next significant world-changing leap forwards.

You can't not embrace change. Because, within our generation, change will be normal and a steady state will feel uncomfortable: you will become acutely conscious of not changing. How do you live a full life?

I had the opportunity recently to listen to David Cameron talking shortly after he had attended a G8 summit in Belfast. He remarked that sitting there, looking around the table at the other leaders, he had realized that there is no pre-ordained destiny that any one country is going to struggle economically, alongside the thought that in that one room you have everyone who can change everything. It only depends on the desire and the will to do it.

I would add to that the need to distil that vision, because if a politician does not get elected they cannot put it into practice, so that vision must be driven down into the populace, just as all the other leaders have to get their visions driven down into the populace.

It is your responsibility to write your own destiny, because if you don't it will be written for you. A new day will begin tomorrow. The world doesn't stop because you haven't written your destiny, but you have the opportunity. It is written by us, and by default if you *don't* write your destiny it will be written for you.

Taking control of my life, which is in essence *taking control of my fears*, allowed me to realize that I could change the direction of my life from that very second onwards.

* *

Do not resign yourself, but embrace the fact that things can never be the same. Enjoy the journey. I had a message printed up – I still have it in my office now – when I was in Denmark. I was the fifth managing director they had had in four years. It was a culture change they needed not a leadership change. No one had done this before.

That was when I dressed up as Father Christmas, to capture the hearts and minds, because the next stage was to impart a vision, but I could not impart the vision until they believed in me, trusted me. That was about going a bit crazy, doing something a bit odd. I have kept letters from employees at the company when I left after three years. "Mike, you changed my life, I am so sad you are leaving."

The point was that it wasn't about delivery, delivery, delivery – that was important of course – but about something more than that. I had large banners made and placed on the flagpoles outside the building. The company was part of ICL, and the flagpoles were meant to fly the ICL flags. I took down the branded flags and put up ones that said instead, "Success is a journey, not a destination." We were saying this to the outside world.

That was a very alien concept, because if you think about the way external companies see you, you want them to think you are successful. That you are going to deliver.

Coming back to our delivery, it's a journey. Have we actually stopped? No we haven't. There is no "stop" here.

"Success is a journey, not a destination. You are constantly achieving it, so you are continuously having to evolve. Otherwise yesterday's success is tomorrow's failure, because if you did tomorrow what you did yesterday it wouldn't be enough."

The future factor #forgetstrategy

@GETRESULTSBOOK

Relish the immense possibilities the future offers

Most conflicts in history have been generated by hate – none have been resolved by hate

Each one of us holds a unique and powerful key, the key to unlock the chains of our past

Don't let your past drag on your future like a ball and chain. Let it go, and then build a new future

The future is unknown: it may be a challenging, fragmented and ungrounded place, but it should never be a frightening place

Nothing lasts for ever, except change – the most valuable asset a leader has is the ability to innovate, constantly

---

ON GROUNDLESS GROUND

"When there are no guiderails, trust in your vision to show you the way forward."

I t was getting late, very late. Possibly too late. I had brought my management team to Iceland. The plan was to hike up an ice glacier – a way of getting everyone on the team to confront a mixture of physical, emotional and mental challenges far outside the normal confines of the office.

We had flown up to Reykjavik but been delayed. We were picked up at the airport and driven straight to this glacier, which from our perspective was in the middle of nowhere. We had no idea where we were, only that the cars had had to go off-road for half an hour to get us to the base of the glacier. There was no one else around, no man-made light, just us.

It was starting to grow dark, because the whole adventure was much, much later than we had anticipated because of the flight delay. The conditions were far from ideal. The guys organizing the expedition were professionals, but there were only two of them, and 15 or 16 of us.

To help us keep a footing on the ice they had issued us with crampons to give us spikes under our shoes. But now they also handed out helmets with torches on as the sun continued to fall.

We set off, walking and walking up this glacier. It was relatively steep. Along the way they were handing out shots of whiskey, or some kind of warming Icelandic liqueur, to keep us warm. The shots helped. When we reached the top of the glacier, the views were spectacular. But now night was descending very fast.

When we turned round, we could not see far. The vehicles that had brought us to the glacier were not visible. Suddenly it felt pitch black, and even with our helmet light we could not see very far. The way down was not marked. There were no guiderails, and on the way up we had seen that in the glacier there were holes two metres across beneath which was a drop of 30 to 40 metres of sheer ice. The chances were that if you slipped into one of the holes, you could kiss your return ticket goodbye, because there was no way the rescue crews could arrive before you died from hypothermia.

It suddenly felt extremely dangerous. I wondered if I had been reckless. But we listened to the guides. They had known the risks of setting off up the glacier at that point in the evening. We trusted them that it was still safe.

But at the top of the glacier, with minimal visibility, gut feeling kicked in. No one really wanted to move. The problem was that we were all at the top of the glacier and we really needed to get back down. If we stayed up there all night we would freeze.

I had a flashback to the Millennium Programme I had been on with ICL. One of the talks I had heard was about something not that far removed from this: an Arctic explorer who had found himself stuck, with a choice of going forward to the next camp or going back to the one he had just come from. A storm was brewing, and he knew if he carried on there was a chance he might never make the other camp. But he also realized that although he knew where the previous camp was, the storm was worse behind him. There was no good solution. But if he stood where he was, he would die for sure. He had to get to one point or the other.

By consciously making the decision to say, "This is what I am going to do and there is no other choice" he persevered and fate, fortune – call it what you want – played on his side. There's a quote I like, from Ralph Waldo Emerson that says, "Once you make a decision, the universe conspires to make it happen."

The visualization of that was the scene in *Indiana Jones and the Last Crusade*, when there is no apparent way across a vast crevasse. He refers to his book of guidance: "Only in the leap of faith will he prove his worth." He takes a step into the void and his boot lands on an invisible bridge. He gains the courage to step out into space and keep walking. On the far side he takes a handful of sand and throws it onto the walkway for the way back.

On the top of the glacier with night closing in, and my entire team looking to me for guidance, I remembered that quote. I knew we all had to overcome our fear to get back down the glacier. Someone had to lead the way. So with the guides I broke the group into teams of three and nominated the person I felt was most confident to be the leader. "You walk and the other two will follow you." I did not make the decision based on any knowledge of their aptitude for ice-climbing, because I had no idea. I based it on my instinct about their confidence. There were real dangers.

The important thing was to make a decision, to do something, to get moving. By breaking them down into groups of three and selecting the most confident person – "One, two, three, go – the rest of you follow in a straight line, don't spread out" – we were taking the initiative. The person leading each small team had no particular skill set for finding the way down the mountain. But I thought they had the confidence to take the next step. The others followed in their footsteps, which offered a route to follow, a trodden path.

We were all treading on groundless ground. Taking the step, making that leap of faith, believing the ice would be there rather than the hole. We all made it down safely.

Reflecting on that experience, I feel it touches on most if not all of the core points in this book.

We all felt **fear** at the top of the glacier, because there was a real chance we might not get back down. But rather than being transfixed by that fear we made the decision to do something – and that gave us a sense of **freedom**: it was up to us to put a plan into action. The key was **flexibility**, not worrying about who was whose boss, but nominating the most confident to lead a team of three back down the glacier.

Failure in this situation was not going to be an option: being prepared to fail opened up a whole new range of options. We trusted our vision of being back at the bottom of the glacier. **Faith**, on the other hand, was paramount – we were walking into unknown territory, standing on "groundless ground" but confident that by taking that decision all the positive element of **fortune** would come into play.

Without a communal sense of **fortitude** – the temperature had plummeted along with the sun – we would never have made it down. Without **focusing** on the positive, subliminally addressing and defeating the negatives, we would not have continued walking. When we made it back to Reykjavik, the release of **fun** was tangible. And by considering that the evening's glacier walk might have been our last moment on earth, the blaze of brightness from the vehicle lights when we reached the bottom represented the fact that the **future** was even brighter.

I tell this story because business is like this. Walking into the darkness, unsure what the next step may hold – *terra firma* or a bottomless pit – relying on teamwork, instinct, confidence and vision.

And if along the way, ten shots, not of whiskey but of the F Factor, help you to take the right path . . . then maybe, just maybe, you will discover the path to outstanding results.

ACKNOWLEDGEMENTS

For **faith**:

Jagdish Parikh for giving me the life tools that have enabled me to endure.

Billy, Gen and John, for putting up with me on my journey to get to where I am.

Holly Bennion and the team at Wiley – especially Jenny Ng, Vicky Kinsman and Megan Saker – for seeing the potential in this book.

Rupert Robson, the most intelligent person I know.

To the old man in Bond Street tube station who told me when I was 19 to always go the extra mile, because there is less traffic there.

My mum, for everything.

For **fortitude**:

James Tyler for being Mr Reliable. A true friend.

Telecity's management team. Simply the best in the world, including my best men Martin and Stéphane.

Philip Dodd, whose persistence and calm has guided me through the process perfectly.

The Telecity board for being there as good counsel.

Friends too numerous to mention, including Niclas S, Richard H, Sam R, Rob C, Luca B, Matt S, Adam S, Alex S, John A and many more.

Winston Churchill – never, never, never give up.

For **fun**:

Eloise, Nelson and Rose for their unconditional love.

Shalina for the great photography in this book.

To all the above for the happiness they give me!

ABOUT
MICHAEL TOBIN

Michael Tobin is CEO of the data centre provider Telecity-Group plc, overseeing an expanding group of businesses across Europe. In October 2007 Michael successfully floated the company on the London Stock Exchange. It is now a major FTSE250 technology stock, the largest operator in its industry sector by revenues in Europe and the fourth provider globally.

His management techniques are both challenging and original. There is little he won't ask his team to try in order to test themselves and encourage them to think differently.

Michael is an acknowledged authority on management techniques and business leadership, regularly speaking at major forums such as TEDx and a frequent contributor on broadcast media including Sky News, CNBC and Newsnight. In the past decade Michael's career has been recognized with numerous awards for his entrepreneurship, leadership and business success. In 2013 he was nominated as Business Leader of the Year in the National Business Awards. In 2014 he was awarded an OBE for services to the Digital Economy.

An amateur magician, Michael devotes significant time and energy to philanthropic endeavours and sits on the fundraising Boards of the Prince's Trust, Action For Children, the Loomba Trust, Make a Wish Foundation and Great Ormond Street Hospital.

Born in Bermondsey, Michael lived and worked abroad for many years. He now lives in London. This is his first book.